this was a man

by Noël Coward

SAMUELFRENCH-LONDON.CO.UK
SAMUELFRENCH.COM

Copyright © 1926 by Noël Coward
All Rights Reserved

THIS WAS A MAN is fully protected under the copyright laws of the United States of America, the British Commonwealth, including Canada, and all other countries of the Copyright Union. All rights, including professional and amateur stage productions, recitation, lecturing, public reading, motion picture, radio broadcasting, television and the rights of translation into foreign languages are strictly reserved.

ISBN 978-0-573-11442-7

Cover image by Elias Quezeda via Flickr.

www.samuelfrench-london.co.uk / www.samuelfrench.com

FOR AMATEUR PRODUCTION ENQUIRIES

UNITED KINGDOM AND EUROPE
plays@SamuelFrench-London.co.uk
020 7255 4302/01

UNITED STATES AND CANADA
info@SamuelFrench.com
1-866-598-8449

Each title is subject to availability from Samuel French, depending upon country of performance.

CAUTION: Professional and amateur producers are hereby warned that *THIS WAS A MAN* is subject to a licensing fee. Publication of this play does not imply availability for performance. Both amateurs and professionals considering a production are strongly advised to apply to the appropriate agent before starting rehearsals, advertising, or booking a theatre. A licensing fee must be paid whether the title is presented for charity or gain and whether or not admission is charged.

The professional rights in this play are controlled by Alan Brodie Representation, The Courtyard, 55 Charterhouse Street, London EC1M 6HA.

No one shall make any changes in this title for the purpose of production. No part of this book may be reproduced, stored in a retrieval system, or transmitted in any form, by any means, now known or yet to be invented, including mechanical, electronic, photocopying, recording, videotaping, or otherwise, without the prior written permission of the publisher. No one shall upload this title, or part of this title, to any social media websites.

The right of Noel Coward to be identified as author of this work has been asserted by him in accordance with Section 77 of the Copyright, Designs and Patents Act 1988

THIS WAS A MAN
A Comedy in Three Acts
Written in 1926

First presented by Basil Dean and the Klaw Theatre, New York, 23 November 1926 (31 performances)

CHARACTERS (In the order of their appearance)

CAROL CHURT	*Francine Larrimore*
HARRY CHALLONER	*Terrence Neill*
EDWARD CHURT	*A. E. Matthew*
LADY MARGOT BUTLER	*Violet Campbell*
BERRY	*Leonard Loan*
LORD ROMFORD	*Mackenzie Ward*
ZOE ST. MERVIN*	*Auriol Lee*
MAJOR EVELYN BATHURST	*Nigel Bruce*
BLACKWELL	*Horace Pollock*
DIRECTOR	*Basil Dean*
DESIGNER	*George W. Harris and G.E Calthrop*

*Spelt Merryn in the published play and in the German version, also in Paris

London premiere presented by Julyan Creative Productions in association with Neil McPherson for the Finborough Theatre, 15 July 2014

EDWARD CHURT	*Jamie De Courcey*
CAROL CHURT	*Dorothea Myer-Bennett*
HARRY CHALLONER	*Alex Corbet Burcher*
LADY MARGOT BUTLER	*Grace Thurgood*
BOBBIE ROMFORD	*Nicholas Audsley*
ZOE ST. MERRYN*	*Georgina Rylance*
MAJOR EVELYN BATHURST	*Robert Portal*
DIRECTOR	*Belinda Lang*
SET AND COSTUME DESIGN	*Simon Kenny*
LIGHTING DESIGN	*Matt Eagland*
SOUND DESIGN	*Max Pappenheim*

PRODUCTION NOTE

To find an almost unknown play by an author you love is exciting. To discover that it had been banned in its day because of its attitude to adultery adds piquancy. To be allowed to adapt it, direct it, and unravel its mysteries is an honour.

When Noel Coward wrote this piece in 1926 he may well have been horrified to imagine that it's London opening would have been not only so very delayed, but on such a small scale and that liberties, however minimal, would have been taken with his script. I have felt an enormous sense of responsibility and though, upon occasion, I have sensed the ghostly presence of a Cowardly wagging finger, I hope that the work that has been done, both before and during the rehearsal period, has remained true to the essence and spirit of the play.

For those of us who have devoured and enjoyed so may of his other works it is fascinating to find parallels and similarities. For those who haven't, I believe this stands alone as an entertaining and interesting study of relationships and betrayal in the aftermath of the Great War, the dialogue and action as fresh and recognisable today as it was then, the characters as flawed and understandable.

I hope that this publication of Noel Coward's original text will enable the play to take its place proudly beside its more popular companions.

Belinda Lang, July 2014

To

John C. Wilson

CHARACTERS

(In the order of their appearance)

EDWARD CHURT
CAROL CHURT
HARRY CHALLONER
MARGOT BUTLER
BERRY
BOBBIE ROMFORD
ZOE ST. MERRYN
MAJOR EVELYN BATHURST
BLACKWELL

ACT I

Scene I. Edward Churt's studio in Knightsbridge – 2.30am.
Scene II. The same. A few weeks later.

ACT II

Scene. Evelyn Bathurst's flat. The same night.

ACT III

Scene. The same as Act I. The following morning.

ACT I

Scene I

EDWARD CHURT's studio in Knightsbridge is furnished with mingled opulence and good taste – he is a successful modern portrait-painter.

When the curtain rises it is about 2.30am. There is a faint glow from the fireplace on the left; a table stands more or less C., upon which is a reading lamp illumining a decanter of whisky, some siphons, a plate of biscuits and another of sandwiches, and two or three glasses; there are also a box of cigarettes and matches. The rest of the room is in comparative darkness. There is the sound of a taxi drawing up in the street, then after a suitable pause the noise of the front door being opened. **CAROL CHURT** *enters, followed by* **HARRY CHALLONER**. *They are both in evening dress.* **CAROL** *is lovely and exquisitely gowned; her vivid personality is composed of a minimum of intellect and a maximum of sex.* **HARRY** *possesses all the earmarks of a social success – he is an excellent ballroom dancer, compared with which his activities in the city are negligible.*

CAROL. Don't make a noise.

HARRY. I wasn't.

CAROL. I didn't say you were – I said don't.

HARRY. All right.

CAROL. Do you want a drink?

HARRY. Yes, please.

CAROL. Help yourself then – and give me one.

She takes of her cloak and lights a cigarette.

HARRY. Say when.
CAROL. That's enough. *(He fills up the glass with soda and hands it to her.)*
HARRY. Here.
CAROL. Thanks.
HARRY. You're a marvel.
CAROL. Why?
HARRY. You're so steady.
CAROL. I don't see any reason for being anything else.
HARRY. You don't think he'll find out?
CAROL. Of course not.
HARRY. Where does he sleep?
CAROL. *(pointing to door, R.)* In there.

HARRY, *with big drink in his hand, tiptoes over and listens at the door.*

HARRY. I can't hear a sound.
CAROL. He doesn't snore unless he's taken to it lately.
HARRY. *(returning)* Darling, do you love me?
CAROL. What a silly question!
HARRY. It's all been so wonderful.
CAROL. *(smiling)* Has it?
HARRY. Well, hasn't it?
CAROL. Yes, it has rather. *(He puts down his drink and takes her in his arms.)* Look out – *(She is holding her glass out at arm's length to prevent it upsetting.)*
HARRY. Put it down, darling – *(There is a good deal of passion in his voice when he says "darling".)*
CAROL. Why?
HARRY. I want to kiss you.
CAROL. Again?
HARRY. Yes, again and again and again – for ever. *(He takes her glass and slams it down on the table.)*
CAROL. Shhh! Don't be a fool.
HARRY. I don't care – *(He kisses her lingeringly.)*

CAROL. *(gently disentangling herself)* I do – it's silly to be reckless.

HARRY. I don't believe you love me as much as you did before.

CAROL. It isn't that at all – you know it isn't.

HARRY. Kiss me then.

CAROL. Very well. *(She goes up to him and quietly kisses him on the mouth. They stand there motionless for a moment.)*

HARRY. I want you – all over again – for the first time.

CAROL. *(stroking his face.)* Darling.

HARRY. I'm crazy about you.

CAROL. You must go home to bed now.

HARRY. Will you telephone me?

CAROL. Yes.

HARRY. First thing?

CAROL. Yes.

HARRY. Promise.

CAROL. Promise.

> *They go out of the door. There is a little whispering in the hall. Then a silence and the sound of the front door closing gently.* **CAROL** *comes back into the studio pensively. She finishes her whisky and soda, takes a biscuit, and flings her cloak over her arm; then she switches off the light and goes slowly off up R. Her door closes. After a slight pause* **EDWARD CHURT** *rises from the big arm-chair by the fire in which he has been sitting with his back to the audience, and goes over to the table. He switches on the lamp again and helps himself to a sandwich; he munches on it thoughtfully for a moment, then with an air of determination picks up the whole plate, switches off the lamp and – retires to his room.*

CURTAIN

ACT I

Scene II

The scene is the same. It is an afternoon a few weeks later about five o'clock.

When the curtain rises, **LADY MARGOT BUTLER** *is seated down stage in a slightly picturesque attitude. She is a good-looking woman of about thirty-five.* **EDWARD** *is working on a sketch of her and is hidden from view behind an easel.*

MARGOT. I'm much more comfortable now, Edward.

EDWARD. Yes, I see you are. Would you mind getting uncomfortable again?

MARGOT. *(rearranging herself)* It *is* a shame. Why do you insist on drawing people in such agonising positions?

EDWARD. It makes them feel they're getting their money's worth. You can rest in a moment and have a cigarette.

MARGOT. Was Violet Netherson pleased with your malicious portrayal of all her worst points?

EDWARD. Delighted. As a matter of fact, it *is* one of the best things I've done.

MARGOT. Yes, but hardly from her point of view. I should never forgive you if you did that to me.

EDWARD. I shall do something much worse if you don't keep still.

MARGOT. What about that cigarette?

EDWARD. Shut up.

MARGOT. All right. *(There is silence for a moment.)* Is that one by the door new?

EDWARD. Yes, it's the Fenwick girl – her mother's convinced that she's a wild woodland type.
MARGOT. St. John's Woodland.
EDWARD. I had a bit of a tussle with her.
MARGOT. I like it.
EDWARD. There now, you can relax. I shan't do any more to-day. (**MARGOT** *rises quickly and strides about.*)
MARGOT. I should be loathe to be a professional model.
EDWARD. There are worse fates I believe. Would you like tea or cocktails or anything?
MARGOT. I should like some tea now and a cocktail later on.
EDWARD. Are you going to stay a long time?
MARGOT. I told Bobbie to pick me up.
EDWARD. *(ringing bell)* How is Bobbie?
MARGOT. Splendid. I'm still mad about him.
EDWARD. That's right.
MARGOT. You don't like him, do you?
EDWARD. I hardly know him.
MARGOT. He's such a darling, and a great comfort to me.
EDWARD. *(standing back and regarding his sketch)* I shall only need one more sitting.
MARGOT. I believe you disapprove of me and Bobbie.
EDWARD. Don't be ridiculous. Why should I?
MARGOT. You must *never* disapprove of things, Edward. It's so second rate.
EDWARD. You don't mean that a bit.
MARGOT. Yes, I do.
EDWARD. You secretly disapprove of the whole affair, yourself, really. That's why you always talk about it so much – to sort of brazen it out and put yourself straight with yourself.
MARGOT. Edward, how *can* you! Anyhow, why shouldn't I talk about it. You all know. Everybody knows.

EDWARD. Reticence as a national quality seems to be on the wane.

MARGOT. What a pompous remark!

EDWARD. Perhaps – but true. *(Enter* **BERRY.***)* Tea please, Berry.

BERRY. Very good, sir.

MARGOT. Lemon with mine, please, Berry.

BERRY. Yes, my lady.

He goes out.

MARGOT. You're an awfully difficult person to know properly.

EDWARD. Am I?

MARGOT. You don't give an inch, do you?

EDWARD. Why should I?

MARGOT. Oh, I don't know. Confidences and discussions of everything make life so much more amusing.

EDWARD. Modern society seems to demand intimacy all in a minute. You all lay bare your private affairs to comparative strangers without a qualm.

MARGOT. Oh, Edward, dear, *we're* not strangers.

EDWARD. We met for the first time six months ago.

MARGOT. It seems *ever* so much more.

EDWARD. You'd told me all about Jim and Bobbie and your exact feelings towards each of them before we'd known each other a month.

MARGOT. It's because you're so sympathetic; you invite confidence.

EDWARD. Nonsense.

MARGOT. You're being perfectly horrid to-day. Has anything happened to upset you?

EDWARD. No, I don't think so.

MARGOT. Well I shan't sit for you again unless you're in a better temper.

EDWARD. Don't be cross.

MARGOT. I'm not cross. I'm hurt.
EDWARD. I think perhaps I do feel a little nervy.
MARGOT. There now, I knew it.
  BERRY *enters with tea.*
EDWARD. Here's tea, anyhow. When Lord Romford calls, Berry, show him straight in, will you?
BERRY. Yes, sir.
EDWARD. You'd better make some cocktails.
BERRY. Very well, sir.
  He goes out.
MARGOT. Do you want lemon or milk?
EDWARD. Neither, thanks. Just plain unvarnished tea.
MARGOT. Is that Katherine Loring? *(Looking at picture.)*
EDWARD. Yes, unfinished.
MARGOT. She always is unfinished. She has a negligible personality, I'm afraid. Here you are. *(She hands him his tea.)*
EDWARD. Thank you.
MARGOT. I hear Zoe's back.
EDWARD. Yes, she rang me up this morning.
MARGOT. Where's she been, exactly?
EDWARD. All over the place.
MARGOT. Who with?
EDWARD. By herself, I believe.
MARGOT. My dear, she must have been with *somebody*. She couldn't have been all alone after all that awful business. She'd have gone mad.
EDWARD. She'll be here soon. You'll be able to ask her about it.
MARGOT. You were engaged to her once, weren't you?
EDWARD. Now then, Margot.
MARGOT. You were. I *know* you were. Carol told me.

EDWARD. Well, as a matter of fact, we weren't actually. We've been friends since we were children and we did discuss marriage at one time, but without great conviction.

MARGOT. I can't understand why she let Kenneth divorce her. Everybody knows –

EDWARD. Zoe wished for her freedom and just went about getting it as quickly as possible.

MARGOT. Well I don't know how she could have faced it. I shouldn't have dared –

EDWARD. You're less independent than she is.

MARGOT. I believe you're going to be horrid again.

    BERRY *enters.*

BERRY. *(announcing)* Lord Romford.

    BOBBIE ROMFORD *enters. He is a nice-looking meaningless young man.*

BOBBIE. Excuse me butting in like this, Churt. *(He and* **EDWARD** *shake hands.)*

EDWARD. We were expecting you. The cocktails will be here in a moment.

BOBBIE. Hallo, Margot! How's the picture going?

MARGOT. It's nearly finished, but Edward won't let me see it. He's been thoroughly soured up all the afternoon.

EDWARD. Margot has been trying to persuade me to brush my hair with her.

BOBBIE. *(puzzled)* Brush your hair?

EDWARD. Yes, metaphorically speaking.

BOBBIE. *(relieved)* Oh, I see.

EDWARD. Hair-brushing is a symbol of girlish confidences. Even the nicest people do it.

MARGOT. Edward shuts up like a clam the moment I try to discuss anything in the least interesting. Where have you been, Bobbie?

BOBBIE. Playing squash with Evie at the Bath Club.

EDWARD. Why didn't you bring him along?

BOBBIE. He said he was coming on later.

MARGOT. I suppose he won.

BOBBIE. Yes; he always does.

Enter **BERRY** *with a tray of cocktails.*

EDWARD. Put them down here, Berry. *(He clears a space on the table.)* Do you want any more tea, Margot?

MARGOT. No thanks.

EDWARD. Take away the remains, then, Berry.

BERRY. Yes, sir. *(He piles the tea things up and takes them out.)*

BOBBIE. I saw your wife in St. James's Street, Churt.

MARGOT. *(eagerly)* Who was she with?

BOBBIE. Harry Challoner.

MARGOT. I love Harry. Don't you, Edward?

EDWARD. Passionately.

MARGOT. I expect they were going to Fanny's. She's got a mah-jong party. She seems to imagine it's a novelty. I ought to be there, really, but I just felt I couldn't bear it – all those hot scented women squabbling over the scores.

BOBBIE. Do you mind if I take a cigarette, Churt?

EDWARD. Of course not. I'm so sorry. *(He hands the box.)* Margot?

MARGOT. Thanks, Edward dear.

BERRY enters.

BERRY. *(announcing)* Mrs. St. Merryn.

ZOE ST. MERRYN *enters. She is beautifully dressed and pleasantly unexaggerated.*

ZOE. Edward! *(She takes both his hands.)* I'm terribly excited at seeing you again.

EDWARD. It's grand, isn't it, after a whole year.

ZOE. I've got so much to say I don't know where to start. *(She sees* **MARGOT.***)* Margot, this is lovely. How are you? *(They kiss.)*

MARGOT. You look divine, darling. Do you know Bobbie?

ZOE. *(shaking hands with him)* Bobbie who?
MARGOT. Romford, dear.
ZOE. *(with a soft glance at* MARGOT*)* Oh, yes, of course. I've heard of you.
MARGOT. *What* have you heard? You must tell me.
ZOE. I can't remember at the moment. Edward, give me a cigarette and a cocktail and tell me all about everything.
EDWARD. *(ministering to her)* Cigarette – cocktail – there.
ZOE. Thank you. Now then –
EDWARD. I don't know where to start any better than you do.
ZOE. How's Carol?
EDWARD. Awfully well.
ZOE. Where is she?
EDWARD. Out. She leads a rather hectic life I'm afraid – matinées, bridge, mah-jong, dancing –
ZOE. You reel off those four harmless occupations as thought they were the most ignoble of human frailties.
EDWARD. I didn't mean to, really.
ZOE. They're wonderful *pis allers* for people who don't do things.
EDWARD. I don't believe in *pis allers*.
ZOE. That's not a virtue; it's just part of your creative equipment.
MARGOT. I want to hear all about your travels, Zoe – where you've been and who with.
ZOE. *(laughing)* It's difficult to remember accurately who I was with all the time. You may rest assured that I had an endless succession of lovers, beginning with an elderly mulatto in Honolulu and finishing with a retired matador in Seville.
EDWARD. I hope you're satisfied, Margot.
MARGOT. Don't be so annoying, Zoe. I really am frightfully interested.

ZOE. You always are, darling, in other people's affairs.
MARGOT. Naturally – they all sound so much more entertaining than my own. Did you see Jim anywhere about in Spain?
ZOE. Yes, in Barcelona. He'd just come in from a yachting cruise.
MARGOT. *(eagerly) Who* was with him? *Do* tell me!
ZOE. Nobody. I met him coming out of a bathroom at the Ritz.
MARGOT. Did he look more or less unattached?
ZOE. Yes. He seemed quite happy.
EDWARD. Margot's interest in her husband is so maternal, it always makes me feel as though I were in the presence of something sacred!
MARGOT. I'm awfully fond of Jim, really – particularly when he's on a yachting cruise.
ZOE. Are you definitely living apart now?
MARGOT. Oh yes – except for religious festivals like Easter and Christmas; then we forgather and go down to Draycott with the children.
EDWARD. *(smiling)* It seems a comfortable arrangement, doesn't it?
ZOE. Frightfully.
MARGOT. *(reflectively)* We *could* get a divorce, I suppose, but it would make such dreary complications. And then when you're free there's the awful danger of starting the whole thing over again with someone else.
ZOE. I haven't noticed it.
MARGOT. You will, I expect, dear – later on. *(She rises.)* I've enjoyed my nice cocktail very much, thank you, Edward. I must go now. Come and lunch on Thursday, Zoe darling. I've only got Rebecca coming. She'll adore seeing you again.
ZOE. All right. One-thirty?
MARGOT. Yes. Come along, Bobbie. Good-bye, Edward. Give my love to Carol.

EDWARD. I will. Good-bye.

BOBBIE. Good-bye.

MARGOT. *(at door)* You've come back from abroad a changed woman, Zoe, if *that's* any comfort to you.

She and **BOBBIE** *go out.*

ZOE. What a sham Margot is, isn't she?

EDWARD. Not really. Just a type.

ZOE. Yes, but she's a type that couldn't exist unless surrounded by false values.

EDWARD. She's making the best of a bad job.

ZOE. She's letting everything slide – morals, dignity, and discretion. Thank heaven, I broke away. I might have got like that.

EDWARD. I wonder if breaking away *is* such a very good plan.

ZOE. Of course it is. It's the most regenerating thing in the world.

EDWARD. You're so dashing, Zoe. Have another cigarette?

ZOE. *(taking one)* Thanks. I feel almost panic-stricken, you know.

EDWARD. Why?

ZOE. Coming back anywhere is always such a dreadful anti-climax.

EDWARD. Not such an anti-climax as staying still.

ZOE. To think that this all used to be my life before I let Kenneth divorce me.

EDWARD. It's pretty futile, isn't it?

ZOE. Futile! I return after a year's oblivion, thrilled and excited, longing to see all my old friends, and what do I find? Clacking shallow nonentities doing the same things, saying the same things, thinking the same things. They're stale. They seem to have lost all wit and charm, and restraint – or perhaps they never had any. Oh dear! I've never felt so depressed in my life.

EDWARD. I hope I haven't let you down, too.

ZOE. No, Edward. You're unchanged; a little dim, perhaps.
EDWARD. Dim?
ZOE. Yes. All your vitality seems to have been snuffed out by something. I expect it's success. That's always frightfully undermining.
EDWARD. Yes, I suppose it is.
ZOE. Are you pleased with everything?
EDWARD. Naturally.
ZOE. I'm sorry.
EDWARD. Why? Oughtn't I to be?
ZOE. You oughtn't to pretend.
EDWARD. Pretend?
ZOE. Yes. You never used to – with me, anyhow.
EDWARD. One gets into the habit of accepting things at their surface value and not looking any deeper.
ZOE. It's a bad habit.
EDWARD. I must pretend. Don't you see?
ZOE. No.
EDWARD. I'm successful – prosperous. I've got everything I wanted.
ZOE. You haven't. You've merely got what other people think you wanted.
EDWARD. *(smiling)* You're wonderfully stimulating, Zoe – like a breath of Brighton air.
ZOE. You look as if you need stimulating, badly.
EDWARD. I do.
ZOE. I'm glad I came back now.
EDWARD. So am I. Devoutly glad.
ZOE. What's wrong?
EDWARD. Lots of things.
ZOE. Carol?
EDWARD. Yes.
ZOE. I thought so.

EDWARD. You were right from the first. It's been a dreary failure.

ZOE. I apologise. It's so irritating being right.

EDWARD. It doesn't irritate me in the least. With anyone else it would, perhaps. But you're different; you always have been.

ZOE. I know you better than most people.

EDWARD. I know you do.

ZOE. What has she been doing?

EDWARD. The obvious thing.

ZOE. I must say I consider marriage an overrated amusement.

EDWARD. I feel rather lost.

ZOE. Yes, I did, too – over Kenneth. It's a nasty feeling.

EDWARD. It's so difficult to know exactly the right attitude to adopt.

ZOE. Are you in love with her still?

EDWARD. I don't know, really. Not violently like at first – that's died down, naturally – but somehow – things get an awful hold on you, don't they?

ZOE. Yes, fortunately for the sanctity of home life.

EDWARD. But the hold ought to be mutual.

ZOE. Quite.

EDWARD. I have moments of fierce rage, you know; then it evaporates, leaving a dead sort of a calm.

ZOE. How long have you known.

EDWARD. Ages, subconsciously; definitely, only a few weeks.

ZOE. Does she know you know?

EDWARD. She hasn't the faintest suspicion. She's always been marvellously self-assured.

ZOE. She's a lovely creature – governed entirely by sex. That's why she's self-assured.

EDWARD. Will she always go on like this?

ZOE. I expect so. Anyhow, as long as she remains attractive – probably after. That's the penalty of her type.

EDWARD. It's beastly, isn't it?

ZOE. Yes, but quite inevitable, I'm afraid. You see she's got no intellect to provide ballast.

EDWARD. Poor Carol.

ZOE. I think you're the one to be considered most at the present moment.

EDWARD. Do you think I ought to have a scene with her about it? I shrink from that. It seems to double the humiliation.

ZOE. I honestly don't know what to say. She's been actually unfaithful to you?

EDWARD. Yes.

ZOE. Often?

EDWARD. *(wearily)* I suppose so. Harry Challoner is in possession at present.

ZOE. Oh dear! How typical.

EDWARD. Everything of that sort is made so much easier for people nowadays. I suppose it's an aftermath of the war.

ZOE. It's the obvious result of this "barriers down" phase through which we seem to be passing. Everyone is at close quarters with everyone else. There's no more glamour. Everything's indefinite and blurred except sex, so people are instinctively turning to that with a rather jaded vigour. It's pathetic when you begin to analyse it.

EDWARD. What fools they all are!

ZOE. *(half smiling)* Has being a success made you realise that?

EDWARD. Yes. There wasn't time before.

ZOE. Why don't you do what I did – go away?

EDWARD. It means sacrificing a good deal of work here in London. I've only just got my foot in, really.

ZOE. Divorce?

EDWARD. I don't feel equal to it at the moment – all the vile publicity, and the lascivious curiosity levelled at Carol and me. It makes me shudder to think of it.

ZOE. For a society portrait-painter you seem unduly sensitive.

EDWARD. If I felt vindictive toward Carol it would be so much easier. But I don't – I merely feel nauseated and frightfully, frightfully bored.

ZOE. The longer you allow it to drift, the worse it will become.

EDWARD. You think I ought to clinch it finally.

ZOE. Yes, I do. Once you've embarked you'll feel better.

EDWARD. No, I shan't

ZOE. I believe you are still in love with her.

EDWARD. No; but I could be again if everything were all right. Oh, Zoe, I loathe this age and everything to do with it. Men of my sort are the products of over-civilisation. All the red-blooded honest-to-God emotions have been squeezed out of us. We're incapable of hating enough or loving enough. When any big moment comes along, good or bad, we hedge round it, arguing, weighing it in the balance of reason and psychology, trying to readjust the values until there's nothing left and nothing achieved. I wish I were primitive enough to thrash Carol and drive her out of my life forever – or strong enough to hold her – but I'm not; I'm just an ass – an intelligent spineless ass! *(He flings himself into a chair and takes a cigarette.)*

ZOE. All the same, being the product of an Age equips you for grappling with it. You've got more chance as you are than, say, Evie Bathurst, for instance.

EDWARD. Evie goes straight for what he wants and gets it.

ZOE. He doesn't demand as much as you.

EDWARD. He's a damned sight happier.

ZOE. I should imagine he misses a good deal.

EDWARD. What does that matter? This situation could never happen to him. He wouldn't let it.
ZOE. You mustn't place too much faith in the strong and silent, Edward. They crumple up quicker than any of us when confronted with something outside their very limited range.
EDWARD. You don't like Evie, do you?
ZOE. You forget I've been married to one of his species.
EDWARD. Evie's not a cad.
ZOE. How do you know?
EDWARD. He could never behave as foully as Kenneth.
ZOE. Kenneth was never anything but an honourable, clean-living Englishman.
EDWARD. He divorced you.
ZOE. Only because I made him.
EDWARD. Why didn't he let you divorce him?
ZOE. It would have been bad for his military career.
EDWARD. You deliberately put yourself in the wrong.
ZOE. Yes.
EDWARD. And you really think it was worth while?
ZOE. Certainly I do. Our natural boredom was verging on hatred – there was no hope of getting back, ever. What's the use of going on with a thing that's dead and done for? I decided to break free.
EDWARD. Is one really happier free?
ZOE. Don't be fatuous, Edward darling.
EDWARD. I don't think I have enough initiative to do anything definite like that.
ZOE. You don't need much initiative. All you've got to do is wait for you opportunity, and grab it!

Enter **BERRY**.

BERRY. *(announcing)* Major Bathurst.

Enter **EVELYN BATHURST**. *He is tall, handsome, soldierly, and essentially masculine. His gaze is frank and correct.* **BERRY** *exits.*

EVELYN. Hullo, Edward! Zoe, I haven't seen you for years. *(They shake hands.)*

ZOE. How are you, Evie?

EVELYN. Splendid! I feel awfully guilty, though. I meant to have written and sympathised over all your beastly divorce business. Will you forgive me?

ZOE. There's nothing to forgive. It was all a howling success, anyway.

EVELYN. Success! Whew! You must have had the hell of a time.

ZOE. It was unpleasant but illuminating.

EDWARD. Want a cocktail, Evie?

EVELYN. No, thanks.

EDWARD. Cigarette?

EVELYN. Rather – yes. *(He takes one.)*

ZOE. How was India?

EVELYN. I don't know. I haven't been there.

ZOE. I'm sorry. I thought you had.

EVELYN. No. Morocco was quite warm enough for me.

ZOE. You arrived at an opportune moment. We were just discussing you.

EVELYN. Good God! What for?

ZOE. Edward was wishing he were more like you.

EVELYN. That's uncommonly nice and right of him. Why this sudden burst of inferiority, Edward?

EDWARD. It's been brewing up for a long time.

EVELYN. *(laughing)* Oh, well, we all come to our senses sooner or later.

ZOE. Not always, Evie.

EVELYN. My only quarrel with Edward is he doesn't take enough exercise.

EDWARD. I'm not very good at exercise.

EVELYN. You never make any effort. Why don't you come and play squash with me sometimes?
EDWARD. That's not exercise, it's flagellation.
EVELYN. He's looking a bit off colour, don't you think, Zoe?
ZOE. Only comparatively.
EVELYN. Been over-working, I suppose?
EDWARD. No, not really.
ZOE. *(rising)* I must go now, Edward.
EVELYN. I shall take it as a personal affront if you leave the moment I arrive.
ZOE. No, you won't, Evie. Good-bye.
EVELYN. *(shaking hands)* Come and have a bit of food sometime.
ZOE. I shuld love to.
EVELYN. Where are you staying?
ZOE. Claridges.
EVELYN. Right. I'll call you up.
ZOE. Good-bye, Edward.
EDWARD. Come again soon, please.
ZOE. Of course. Telephone me to-morrow morning.
EDWARD. I will.
ZOE. Give my love to Carol.

> **EVELYN** *opens the door for her and she goes out.* **EDWARD** *stands looking after her thoughtfully.*

EVELYN. *(sitting down again)* Extraordinary woman, Zoe.
EDWARD. Why extraordinary?
EVELYN. I don't know. She's so self-assured.
EDWARD. *(absently)* Yes. I think she has every reason to be.
EVELYN. She faced all that divorce business very pluckily. Kenneth seems to have behaved like a pretty average swine.
EDWARD. Yes.
EVELYN. Why on earth did she ever marry him?
EDWARD. *(wearily)* Why does anyone ever marry anyone?

EVELYN. I've never felt the urge very strongly. I suppose I've seen too much of it.
EDWARD. That doesn't make any difference, really.
EVELYN. Women are so damned complicated to live with – 'specially Zoe's sort.
EDWARD. I don't think Zoe is particularly complicated. She's always appeared to me to be pretty clear-headed and direct.
EVELYN. Oh well, you know her better than I do.
EDWARD. You're wonderfully single-minded, aren't you?
EVELYN. Single-minded?
EDWARD. Yes. You live according to formulated codes, and you never try to look either under or over them. I do envy you.
EVELYN. You needn't. I have my ups and downs.
EDWARD. Do you, really? Ever since we were at school I've always regarded you as being quite invulnerable.
EVELYN. *(complacently)* Don't be a fool, old man.
EDWARD. I suppose it's a remnant of hero worship.
EVELYN. Rot! I'm a bit more balanced than you, that's all.
EDWARD. That wouldn't be very difficult.
EVELYN. I came here to-day with a purpose. I'm a bit worried. I want to talk to you seriously.
EDWARD. What about?
EVELYN. Lots of things.
EDWARD. All right. Go on.
EVELYN. I don't know how to start, quite; it's difficult.
EDWARD. Why difficult?
EVELYN. Well, you're a bit touchy at times, aren't you?
EDWARD. What's the matter, Evie?
EVELYN. Nothing actually yet – at least, I hope not.
EDWARD. I know what you're driving at.
EVELYN. Do you?
EDWARD. Yes.

EVELYN. Are you sure you do?
EDWARD. People have been talking about Carol, I suppose?
EVELYN. Exactly.
EDWARD. Well, you needn't worry.
EVELYN. I shouldn't, ordinarily, but somehow in this case it's different.
EDWARD. No, it isn't; it's exactly the same; it's a situation that occurs over and over again with everybody. That's why it's such a bore.
EVELYN. That's a silly sort of attitude to take up.
EDWARD. No sillier than any other.
EVELYN. Aren't you going to do anything?
EDWARD. O God! *(He turns away.)*
EVELYN. Well, you'll have to sooner or later.
EDWARD. What is there to do?
EVELYN. Read the riot act.
EDWARD. Do you seriously imagine that that's in any way a final solution?
EVELYN. It ought to bring her to her senses a bit, if you did it with conviction.
EDWARD. That's the trouble. I haven't got a conviction.
EVELYN. Hang it all man, she is your wife!
EDWARD. I am not a man of property.
EVELYN. How do you mean?
EDWARD. I mean I can't look on Carol as a sort of American trunk.
EVELYN. *(exasperated)* What *are* you talking about?
EDWARD. She's a human being, not an inanimate object over which I can assert legal rights.
EVELYN. If all husbands adopted that tone, England would be in a nice state.
EDWARD. It *is* in a nice state.
EVELYN. You make me tired sometimes, Edward.
EDWARD. I expect I do, but it can't be helped.

EVELYN. Yes, it can.
EDWARD. How?
EVELYN. Pull yourself together; show a little spirit.
EDWARD. I suppose you think that if I grabbed Carol by the hair of the head and banged her about and hurled abuse at her, she'd fall at my feet in ecstasies of adoration?
EVELYN. I shouldn't be surprised. Anyhow, it probably would do her good.
EDWARD. For an upstanding British soldier you have an astounding sense of the theatre.
EVELYN. Oh, you can think me a red-blooded savage if you like, but I'm damned if I'd sit down quietly and let my wife make a fool of me.
EDWARD. *(gently)* You haven't got a wife, Evie. If you had you'd probably be utterly vanquished quicker than anyone.
EVELYN. Not me. I know the game too well.
EDWARD. Only from looking on, though. That makes an enormous difference.
EVELYN. Look here, Edward. Why not be sensible about all this?
EDWARD. I am, really.
EVELYN. Nonsense!
EDWARD. It's no use, Evie. Things will have to take their own course.
EVELYN. *(contemptuously)* Line of least resistance, eh?
EDWARD. Yes.
EVELYN. To hell with the line of least resistance.
EDWARD. She can't help herself; she's made like that.
EVELYN. Rubbish!
EDWARD. It isn't rubbish. She's the sort of woman who must attract people all the time. One conquest isn't enough; she must go on and on.

EVELYN. You talk as though she were only just flirting about for the fun of the thing.
EDWARD. Perhaps she is.
EVELYN. What's the use of blinding yourself?
EDWARD. Oh, shut up, Evie!
EVELYN. This is more serious than you think.
EDWARD. No, it isn't.
EVELYN. What do you feel – honestly?
EDWARD. I've told you – bored.
EVELYN. That's not true.
EDWARD. All right.
EVELYN. I know it isn't. We haven't been pals all these years for nothing. You can't deceive me as easily as that.
EDWARD. What do you want me to feel, exactly?
EVELYN. You've got to *do* something.
EDWARD. What?
EVELYN. If you don't, I shall.
EDWARD. Evie, if you mention one word of all this to Carol or anyone in the world, I'll never forgive you.
EVELYN. You needn't worry. I've got a better plan than talking.
EDWARD. What is it?
EVELYN. Leave it to me.
EDWARD. Evie –
EVELYN. She ought to be taught a lesson.
EDWARD. What sort of lesson?
EVELYN. She wants some of the self-assurance knocked out of her.
EDWARD. *(smiling)* Really, Evie!
EVELYN. She needs humiliating.
EDWARD. You're positively vindictive.
EVELYN. Perhaps I am, but it's for your sake.
EDWARD. I'd no idea you disliked Carol so heartily.

EVELYN. It isn't that at all. I don't like or dislike her. She never pays any attention to me, anyhow.
EDWARD. To think there's even a streak of feminine in you!
EVELYN. What do you mean?
EDWARD. Never mind.
EVELYN. I won't stand by and see you let down all along the line.
EDWARD. It's awfully sweet of you, Evie, to be so cross, but you really mustn't be. I'm the one to get cross if necessary.
EVELYN. It is necessary.
EDWARD. You must allow me to be the best judge of that.
EVELYN. Now look here, Edward —
EDWARD. Remember, what I said – you're not to interfere. It's my affair, and mine alone.
EVELYN. I know a good deal more about women, than you.
EDWARD. Do you, Evie?
EVELYN. I've handled too many of them not to.
EDWARD. How mechanical that sounds. *(He laughs.)*
EVELYN. Oh, you're hopeless.

The door opens and CAROL *comes in. She is, as usual, looking delightful.*

CAROL. Hallo, Evie! *(She shakes hands with him.)* Are there any telephone messages for me, Edward.
EDWARD. No.
CAROL. *(taking off her gloves)* I'm quite exhausted.
EDWARD. Where have you been?
CAROL. Playing mah-jong with Fanny. I won a good deal.
EVELYN. Splendid.
CAROL. How's Margot's picture going?
EDWARD. It's nearly finished.
CAROL. Give me a cigarette, Evie.
EVELYN. *(handing her a cigarette)* You look remarkably fit, Carol.

CAROL. *(smiling)* I am fit, but I'm a tiny bit worried over Edward.
EVELYN. Why, he looks all right to me.
CAROL. You don't know him like I do. I can always tell when he's tired and overworked, can't I, darling?
EDWARD. Yes, I'm sure you can.
CAROL. It's all these people buzzing round him all day. Let's go away, Edward, and have a real holiday – somewhere quiet.
EVELYN. That's a damned good idea.
EDWARD. *(smiling)* I can't – for the next six weeks, anyhow.
CAROL. *(with a slight shrug)* There you see? It's quite impossible to do anything with him.
EVELYN. Why don't you chuck everything, and just go?
EDWARD. Funnily enough, Zoe suggested that this afternoon.
CAROL. Zoe? I didn't know she was back.
EDWARD. She arrived yesterday.
CAROL. Why didn't you tell me?
EDWARD. I didn't know until this morning. She rang me up.
CAROL. Well, she didn't lose much time anyhow.
EDWARD. I don't see why she should.
CAROL. I suppose she talked and talked and talked as usual.
EDWARD. Yes, we both talked a good bit.
CAROL. What about?
EDWARD. Everything.
CAROL. No wonder you look tired.
EVELYN. She looked awfully well.
CAROL. She always does. She's wonderfully healthy.
EDWARD. *(with a faint malice)* She sent you her love.
CAROL. *(bored)* Oh – give her mine when she rings up again.
EDWARD. You'll see her to-night at the Harringtons'.

CAROL. No I shan't. I'm not going. They're going to have that awful string quartette again. I suffered so acutely last time.

EDWARD. I shall go by myself, then.

CAROL. Never mind. You'll be able to talk to Zoe.

EDWARD. Where are you dining?

CAROL. With the Challoners at the Embassy; then we're going on somewhere.

EDWARD. Do you want the car?

CAROL. No. They're picking me up.

EDWARD. Right. I'll go and dress. Don't go, Evie. We might have a slight aperitif at one of your disreputable clubs before dinner.

CAROL. Are you dining together?

EDWARD. No. I'm going to the Russian Ballet with Richard and Sheila. They've got a box or something.

EDWARD *goes off into his bedroom.*

EVELYN. You're looking charming, Carol.

CAROL. *(raising her eyebrows)* Thank you.

EVELYN. That's a splendid hat. Is it new?

CAROL. No – incredibly old.

EVELYN. Well, it doesn't look it.

CAROL. I'm glad. *(She goes towards the door.)*

EVELYN. Carol –

CAROL. *(turning)* Yes?

EVELYN. Nothing.

CAROL. *(surprised)* Is there anything the matter?

EVELYN. No – honestly it's nothing.

CAROL. Oh well, I must go and dress, too. See you later on.

EVELYN. I shall be gone when you come down.

CAROL. Really, Evie, you're behaving very strangely.

EVELYN. Why?

CAROL. I don't know. You seem different, somehow.

EVELYN. Won't you stay and talk for a moment. I haven't seen you to speak to for ages.

CAROL. That's your fault.

EVELYN. You're always so engaged.

CAROL. I never seem to have a minute for anything. I *do* wish life wasn't so hectic.

EVELYN. Why do you let it be?

CAROL. I don't. It just happens like that.

EVELYN. I'd resent it a good deal if you were my wife.

CAROL. *(smiling)* Aren't you glad I'm not, Evie?

EVELYN. I don't know.

CAROL. *(surprised)* Well, now! I thought you disliked me thoroughly.

EVELYN. Disliked you?

CAROL. Yes. You always have such a polite, pre-occupied air with me. It makes me feel terribly frivolous and shallow.

EVELYN. How can you, Carol?

CAROL. *(gaily)* It's true. You're the kind of man who despises women dreadfully – I know you are.

EVELYN. You're quite wrong. I adore them.

CAROL. Well, that's a lovely surprise, isn't it?

EVELYN. I can't get over you imagining that I disliked you.

CAROL. I expect it's because you're so tremendously fond of Edward. One always feels that with one's husband's friends.

EVELYN. I don't see any reason, just because I like Edward, that –

CAROL. Don't you, Evie?

EVELYN. Of course not.

CAROL. Well, I'm very, very glad.

EVELYN. That's settled then, isn't it?

CAROL. Quite. I shan't be frightened of you any more.

EVELYN. Frightened of me. How ridiculous!

CAROL. It isn't ridiculous; it's quite natural.
EVELYN. I don't see why. I'm perfectly harmless.
CAROL. Are you?
EVELYN. Mild as a kitten.
CAROL. I wonder.
EVELYN. To think you've been building up the most frightful image of me in your mind all this time and I never knew.
CAROL. You can't blame me, really.
EVELYN. Yes, I can. It's awfully suspicious and distrustful of you.
CAROL. It's your own fault, for holding so aloof.
EVELYN. I don't hold aloof a bit.
CAROL. You've never talked anything but commonplaces to me ever since I've known you.
EVELYN. You never gave me the chance.
CAROL. What did you expect me to do?
EVELYN. I don't know. Just be nice.
CAROL. Haven't I been nice? I'm so sorry.
EVELYN. Yes, I suppose you have, really, but I've always felt you thought me rather dull.
CAROL. You have been – up to now.
EVELYN. *(despondently)* There you are, then!
CAROL. *(quietly)* I said "up to now".
EVELYN. Men of my sort are all wrong in society. We don't seem to fit in, somehow.
CAROL. Are you glad or sorry?
EVELYN. Well, to be frank, I'm glad, until moments like this crop up.
CAROL. You're awfully funny you know.
EVELYN. Funny?
CAROL. Yes. You do despise women, after all.
EVELYN. How do you mean?

CAROL. You think we only like men who play up and talk well and dance well.
EVELYN. It's only natural that you should.
CAROL. Oh no, it isn't.
EVELYN. You think there's some hope for me, after all, then?
CAROL. Now you're fishing.
EVELYN. It's cruel of you to snap me up like that.
CAROL. I'm sorry, Evie.
EVELYN. You'd find me an awful bore after a bit, you know.
CAROL. Why should I?
EVELYN. I take things so damned seriously.
CAROL. That's refreshing! Most of the men I know don't take things seriously enough.
EVELYN. What an extraordinary woman you are!
CAROL. Why extraordinary?
EVELYN. Making me talk like this. I never have before.
CAROL. I shall take that as a compliment, whether you like it or not.
EVELYN. I mean it.
CAROL. Yes, I know you do.
EVELYN. I see now why your life's so hectic and why everyone runs after you so much.
CAROL. *(smiling)* Why?
EVELYN. You've got the most amazing knack of drawing people out.
CAROL. Not always. Only people I like.
EVELYN. You've made me feel lonely for the first time in my life.
CAROL. How hateful of me!
EVELYN. It's not your fault; it's mine.
CAROL. In what way?
EVELYN. I ought to make more efforts and not be so boorish.

CAROL. You're not in the least boorish.

EVELYN. Yes, I am – utterly wrapped up in my own affairs, then suddenly someone like you comes along and makes me realise all in a minute what a lot I'm missing.

CAROL. You're not missing much, really. It's much better to remain yourself than try to be something you're not.

EVELYN. It's awfully sweet of you to say that.

CAROL. I mean it honestly. You can never guess how tired I get by having the same sort of things said to me always.

EVELYN. Do you really?

CAROL. Of course.

EVELYN. I wish you weren't dining out to-night.

CAROL. Why?

EVELYN. I'd like better than anything in the world for you come and dine with me quietly.

CAROL. I'd adore to, Evie, but, you see –

EVELYN. Oh, I know, you can't possibly; but it seems hard that the moment I begin to get to know you properly you're whisked out of sight again.

CAROL. *(gently)* There are lots of other nights.

EVELYN. Yes, I suppose there are.

CAROL. I'm certainly not frightened of you any more now – you're an absolute baby.

EVELYN. Crying for the moon?

CAROL. I don't rate myself quite so high as that.

EVELYN. You're just as unattainable.

CAROL. Evie!

EVELYN. I'm sorry. I oughtn't to have said that.

CAROL. *(after a slight pause)* I don't mind.

EVELYN. You are a dear.

CAROL. Am I?

EVELYN. May I ring you up to-morrow morning?

CAROL. Of course.

EVELYN. And perhaps – sometime soon – ?

CAROL. *(with determination)* I'll dine with you to-night, Evie.
EVELYN. Carol!
CAROL. Yes. I can put off the Challoners. They bore me stiff, anyway. I'd much rather talk to you.
EVELYN. I say, it's most terribly sweet of you to take pity on me like this.
CAROL. Don't be silly. It'll be a mutual benefit. I'm bored and you're bored. Where shall we dine?
EVELYN. Anywhere you choose.
CAROL. The awful thing is I simply daren't go anywhere where I'm likely to be seen.
EVELYN. We could dine at the flat if you like, but it will be fearfully dull.
CAROL. Oh, *let's* do that. And we can creep out somewhere afterward if we feel like it.
EVELYN. Are you sure that's all right?
CAROL. Positive. It will be divine being quiet for once.
EVELYN. Don't say anything to Edward.
CAROL. *(quickly)* Why not?
EVELYN. Well, I got out of dining with him to-night. I wanted to be by myself, you see.
CAROL. Well, you're not going to be now.
EVELYN. I know. Isn't it damnable?
CAROL. Beastly. Will you fetch me?
EVELYN. Yes. What time?
CAROL. Latish – about nine.
EVELYN. Splendid –

Enter **EDWARD** *in evening dress.*

CAROL. You have been quick.
EDWARD. I've hurried. I know how impatient Evie is. Are you quite determined about the Harringtons, Carol?
CAROL. *Quite!* I simply couldn't bear it.
EDWARD. Oh, all right, then. I'll apologise for you.

CAROL. Do, there's a dear. Good-bye, Evie. Come and see me again soon.

EVELYN. Thanks. I will.

EDWARD. Come on. I haven't got much time. Good-night Carol.

CAROL. Good-night, darling.

EDWARD and EVELYN go off. CAROL lights a cigarette and goes to the telephone.

(at telephone) Mayfair 7065 please… Yes. *(A pause)* Hallo! Is that you, Fay… Yes. Can I speak to Harry? Oh yes, rather. I'll hold on… Harry… Yes, it's me. Look here, I can't dine to-night, because I can't, I feel too tired. I may not have looked tired this afternoon, but I tell you I am now… Don't be so annoying, Harry… No, it isn't that at all. I'm going to dine in bed… No, don't. I shall probably be asleep… Well, of course, if you're going to talk like that… I'm afraid you're developing into a bore, Harry. I'm so sorry! *(She bangs down the receiver)* Silly fool!

She picks up her bag and gloves and goes off.

CURTAIN

ACT II

The scene is **EVELYN BATHURST**'s *flat. It is a manly apartment, furnished with precision but no imagination. There is a door up L. opening into a small hall and thence to the front door. Up R. is* **EVIE**'s *bedroom and down L. a service door. Between these two is the fireplace, in front of which is a large sofa and a couple of armchairs. The windows occupy the right wall. The table, C., is laid for two.*

When the curtain rises, it is about 9.15pm and **BLACKWELL** *is putting the finishing touches, which consist of a bowl of roses and a bottle of champagne in an ice bucket. He is regarding his handiwork pensively when there comes the sound of a key in the front door. After a moment* **EVELYN** *and* **CAROL** *enter.* **EVELYN** *is wearing a dinner jacket;* **CAROL**, *an elaborately simple dinner dress and cloak.*

CAROL. What a nice flat!

EVELYN. I've been here for years.

CAROL. It's all quite typical of you.

EVELYN. How do you know?

CAROL. Well, don't you think it is?

EVELYN. I've never thought about it much.

CAROL. Solid and rather austere.

EVELYN. That sounds beastly.

CAROL. No. I like it.

EVELYN. I'm glad. Let me take your cloak. *(He takes her cloak and lays it over a chair.)* Cocktails please, Blackwell.

BLACKWELL. Yes, sir. *(He goes off.)*

CAROL. I suppose he's been with you as long as the flat?

EVELYN. Longer, really; he was my batman when I was a raw subaltern.
CAROL. *(smiling)* You must have been rather nice as a subaltern.
EVELYN. Oh no, I wasn't. You ask Edward.
CAROL. Edward adores you.
EVELYN. We're very old friends.
CAROL. It's always puzzled me. You're so very different from each other.
EVELYN. Edward's a damn sight cleverer.
CAROL. Now then –
EVELYN. But he is.
CAROL. You seem to have done very well at your job and you're always winning things.
EVELYN. I haven't done anything.
CAROL. Nonsense. *(She wanders round the room, looking at photographs.)* Who's this?
EVELYN. Mary Liddle. I was engaged to her once.
CAROL. Oh, I see.
EVELYN. I suppose you want to know why nothing ever came of it.
CAROL. Of course.
EVELYN. She ran off with someone she hardly knew.
CAROL. What a shame!
EVELYN. I expect I bored her stiff –
CAROL. Were you very much in love with her?
EVELYN. Yes. I think I was.
CAROL. I can't imagine you in love.
EVELYN. It doesn't happen often.
CAROL. *(smiling and patting his arm)* Never mind, Evie.
EVELYN. I don't. It's a relief really.

 BLACKWELL *enters with the cocktails; they both take them.*

 Dinner please, Blackwell.

BLACKWELL. Very good, sir. *(He goes out.)*
CAROL. *(at another photograph)* Is this your mother?
EVELYN. Yes.
CAROL. You're awfully like her.
EVELYN. It's the nose, I think.
CAROL. And the chin – so firm and unrelenting. I love firm chins.
EVELYN. They're awfully deceptive.
CAROL. *(sipping her cocktail)* Are they, Evie?
EVELYN. Yes. I'm weak as water, really.
CAROL. You'll have to prove it to me before I believe it.
EVELYN. I'd rather not.
> **BLACKWELL** *enters with caviare.*

Come and sit down.
CAROL. *(sitting at table)* What divine roses!
EVELYN. They're in your honour.
CAROL. Thank you. I hoped they were. *(***BLACKWELL** *helps her to caviare.)*
EVELYN. *(opening champagne)* I feel awfully flattered at your being here.
CAROL. Why should you?
EVELYN. I just do.
CAROL. Don't be silly. *(He fills her glass and his own.)* Thanks.
EVELYN. I feel flattered because it's something I never thought possible.
CAROL. Me dining with you?
EVELYN. Yes.
CAROL. Idiot. *(She smiles.)*
EVELYN. I've always seen you as a frightfully dazzling creature – always in demand – always rushing about.
CAROL. Just because you feel flattered yourself, you mustn't begin to flatter me.
EVELYN. Is that flattery?

CAROL. Isn't it?
EVELYN. Well yes, and no.
CAROL. You mean you've never quite approved of me.
EVELYN. I didn't say that.
CAROL. I believe it's true, all the same.
EVELYN. I've wondered a bit what you were really like.
CAROL. *(with subtle pathos)* I don't think I know, myself.
EVELYN. You haven't had much time to think, have you?
CAROL. No – I suppose not.
EVELYN. *(sententiously)* We're all so different underneath.
CAROL. *(laughing)* Oh, Evie!
EVELYN. What?
CAROL. You're awfully serious!
EVELYN. Don't laugh at me.
CAROL. I wasn't –
EVELYN. I don't mind, really; it shows that you're enjoying yourself.
CAROL. I am thoroughly.
EVELYN. I was terrified that you'd be bored.
CAROL. You're fishing again.
EVELYN. I wish you weren't so quick; it embarrasses me. *(He laughs).*
CAROL. I'll try to be slower. *(She laughs too.)*
EVELYN. I'm the plodding sort, you know – gets there in the end, but takes a long time about it.
CAROL. Nonsense!
EVELYN. The British army doesn't specialise in wit.
CAROL. I won't hear a word against the British army.
EVELYN. *(with jocularity)* Hurrah! *(They both laugh.)*
CAROL. You're like a schoolboy.
EVELYN. I feel like one with you.
CAROL. Do I look so terribly old?
EVELYN. You know I didn't mean that.
CAROL. I'll let you off this time, but you mustn't do it again.

BLACKWELL *enters with the soup; he takes away the caviare plates.*
EVELYN. How long is it since you dined quietly like this?
CAROL. Oh, ages.
EVELYN. I thought so.
CAROL. You're looking disapproving again.
BLACKWELL *serves the soup and exits.*
EVELYN. I think I'm envious.
CAROL. Envious?
EVELYN. Yes.
CAROL. No, you're not, really.
EVELYN. Your life would never suit me, I know, but somehow it does sound rather fun, for a change.
CAROL. Let's make a bargain.
EVELYN. I know what you're going to say.
CAROL. Change over for a bit.
EVELYN. Temptress.
CAROL. You come out to a few theatres and parties with me –
EVELYN. I can't dance well enough.
CAROL. I'll soon teach you.
EVELYN. I'd drive you mad.
CAROL. Have you a gramophone here?
EVELYN. Yes.
CAROL. We'll start after dinner.
EVELYN. All right.
CAROL. And whenever I'm tired and sick of everything, I'll come here and dine quietly like this.
EVELYN. Will you, honestly?
CAROL. Of course, if you stick to your side of the compact.
EVELYN. I don't believe you'll have the patience to carry it through.
CAROL. You must despise me.

EVELYN. Despise you? Good heavens! Why?
CAROL. You're so untrusting.
EVELYN. No, I'm not; but it does look as though I were going to get more out of this than you.
CAROL. Not at all. It's a perfectly fair exchange. You've no idea how utterly weary I get every now and then.
EVELYN. Poor Carol.
CAROL. This is peace, absolute peace, and I'm tremendously grateful to you for it. *(They look at each other in silence for a moment.* EVELYN*'s expression is faintly nonplussed.)*
EVELYN. The compact's on.
CAROL. Good! Shake hands.
EVELYN. Right you are. *(They shake hands across the table.* CAROL *allows hers to remain in his a shade more than is strictly necessary.)*
CAROL. Do you want to come to the first night of *Round Pegs* on Thursday?
EVELYN. What on earth's that?
CAROL. A new play by Burton Trask.
EVELYN. Who's he?
CAROL. *(laughing)* Oh, Evie!
EVELYN. Well, how should I know?
CAROL. He's only the most talked of dramatist we've got.
EVELYN. Sorry.
CAROL. He wrote *The Sinful Spinster.*
EVELYN. Oh, the play all the fuss was about last year.
CAROL. Yes.
EVELYN. It sounded pretty hot stuff.
CAROL. It wasn't, really, but the woman in it fell in love with a man younger than herself and the Church of England didn't like it.
EVELYN. Oh, I see!
CAROL. You need educating badly.
EVELYN. I'm afraid I do.

BLACKWELL *enters and takes away their soup plates.*

CAROL. Wasn't it funny us talking this afternoon and you asking me to dine all in a minute?

EVELYN. Awfully funny, but very lucky for me.

CAROL. You make me feel shy when you say things like that. It was just as lucky for me.

EVELYN. *(with intensity)* Was it, honestly?

CAROL. *(looking down)* Of course.

BLACKWELL *enters with partridges and attendant vegetables. He serves them during the ensuing dialogue.*

EVELYN. Edward's looking awfully tired these days.

CAROL. *(absently)* Is he? I haven't noticed it.

EVELYN. Why, you said so yourself this afternoon.

CAROL. So I did. I remember he looked very wan when I came in. By the way, what were you two discussing so intently. I felt as though I were interrupting a Masonic meeting.

EVELYN. Nothing particular.

CAROL. Me, by any chance?

EVELYN. Good heavens, no!

CAROL. There's no need to be so vehement about it; it wouldn't have mattered if you had been.

EVELYN. Have some more champagne.

CAROL. Thanks – just a little. *(She holds out her glass and he fills it, also his own)*

EVELYN. *(with great boldness)* Why did you think we were talking about you?

CAROL. You both looked so guilty.

EVELYN. Surely that proves we weren't.

CAROL. Very good, Evie.

EVELYN. You're embarrassing me dreadfully.

CAROL. Am I? Why?

EVELYN. Because we *were* discussing you.

CAROL. Ah!

EVELYN. I see it's useless to try and deceive you for a moment.
CAROL. What were you saying?
EVELYN. Must I tell you?
CAROL. Certainly.
EVELYN. You're terribly unrelenting.
CAROL. Come on – out with it.
EVELYN. I was lecturing Edward.

    BLACKWELL *goes out.*

CAROL. Lecturing him?
EVELYN. Yes. I said he was paying too much attention to his work and not enough to you.
CAROL. And do you think that's true?
EVELYN. Yes.
CAROL. It isn't; it's the other way round, really. I neglect Edward. You should have saved your lecture for me.
EVELYN. I'm sure it's his fault, really, he's so damned lackadaisical.
CAROL. It was nice of you, but a little interfering.
EVELYN. I'm sorry. I suppose I deserve to be snubbed.
CAROL. I'm not snubbing you, exactly, but I'm puzzled.
EVELYN. Why puzzled?
CAROL. It seems so strange that you should have taken up the cudgels on my side.
EVELYN. That was how I saw the situation.
CAROL. I never realised that there was a situation.
EVELYN. There isn't, but there may be soon
CAROL. How horrid of you!
EVELYN. I know Edward pretty well, you know.
CAROL. And me hardly at all.
EVELYN. Exactly. That's why I went to him, as I told you this afternoon. I always felt that you disliked me and thought me dull.
CAROL. How absurd!

EVELYN. You did, all the same. You'd have crushed me to the earth if I'd dared mention the subject to you.
CAROL. You must have thought me a prig.
EVELYN. Not in the least. I quite saw your point.
CAROL. And now –
EVELYN. Now I'm muddled.
CAROL. Have I muddled you, Evie?
EVELYN. Yes, terribly.
CAROL. I'm so glad.
EVELYN. That's malicious of you.
CAROL. Go ahead with your lecture.
EVELYN. Certainly not.
CAROL. Whose fault do you consider this slight drifting apart – Edward's or mine?
EVELYN. Edward's.
CAROL. I told you it was mine.
EVELYN. I don't believe you.
CAROL. Stubborn.
EVELYN. Is it yours?
CAROL. Yes.
EVELYN. Why?
CAROL. *(seriously)* Oh, Evie –
EVELYN. Tell me.
CAROL. It's rather difficult.
EVELYN. I'm awfully sympathetic.
CAROL. I believe you are
EVELYN. You love him still, don't you?
CAROL. Yes – in a way.
EVELYN. But not so much as you did?
CAROL. Not quite so much.
EVELYN. I suppose that's inevitable in married life, always.
CAROL. I expect it is.
EVELYN. It's sad though.
CAROL. Not if one isn't sentimental about it.

EVELYN. Are you ever sentimental about anything?
CAROL. *(wistfully)* Do I seem so hard?
EVELYN. A little, I think.
CAROL. I'm not, really.
EVELYN. I'm afraid Edward's unhappy.
CAROL. Not deep down inside.
EVELYN. Are you sure?
CAROL. He may think he is.
EVELYN. Poor Edward.
CAROL. He doesn't love me quite so much, either, you know.
EVELYN. Perhaps he wants to, but you won't let him.
CAROL. Evie, why are we talking like this?
EVELYN. I don't know.
CAROL. I can't bear to pretend about things.
EVELYN. You're quite right; it doesn't pay in the long run.
CAROL. But I don't want you to blame Edward and lecture him for something that's not entirely his fault,
EVELYN. I see.
CAROL. I'm awfully fond of him and I always shall be, but –
EVELYN. But what?
CAROL. Don't let's say any more about it.
EVELYN. All right. You're rather a dear, you know.
CAROL. Am I?
EVELYN. More than I ever suspected!
CAROL. Oh, Evie!

> *They look at each other for a moment,* **EVELYN** *intently.* **CAROL** *with a faintly wistful smile.* **BLACKWELL** *enters to collect the plates and serve the sweet – pêche Melba – which he does during ensuing dialogue.*

EVELYN. You don't like Zoe St. Merryn, do you?
CAROL. Why do you suddenly ask that?
EVELYN. I felt you didn't this afternoon.
CAROL. She's rather obvious, I think.

EVELYN. In what way?
CAROL. She tries to be clever.
EVELYN. I always thought she was clever.
CAROL. Yes, most men do, but very few women,
EVELYN. Why is that?
CAROL. Because they see through her. All that divorce business was a put-up job.
EVELYN. I say, Carol!
CAROL. Don't look so shocked. Of course it was. She's been so brave and defiant over it. Men love that.
EVELYN. Aren't you being a little hard on her?
CAROL. No, not really. I know her type so well.
EVELYN. She's an old friend of Edward's, isn't she?
CAROL. Yes, but that hasn't anything to do with it. She tried to marry him once.
EVELYN. He seems very fond of her,
CAROL. She flatters him terribly. He's an awful baby.
EVELYN. Thank heaven I haven't got your feminine intuition. It must complicate life dreadfully.
CAROL. It's very useful sometimes.
EVELYN. Do you size up everyone so mercilessly.
CAROL. *(laughing)* Perhaps.
EVELYN. I'm trembling visibly.
CAROL. Nonsense! You're not frightened by anything, really.
EVELYN. You don't know!

    BLACKWELL *goes out.*

CAROL. Well, you shouldn't be, anyhow.
EVELYN. That's different.
CAROL. Why did you ask me not to tell Edward I was dining with you?
EVELYN. *(nonplussed)* Did I?
CAROL. You know you did.

EVELYN. Perhaps I was afraid he'd think I was interfering again.
CAROL. Did he tell you that, too?
EVELYN. Yes.
CAROL. *(smiling)* Never mind.
EVELYN. I don't. I'm used to Edward.
CAROL. So am I.
EVELYN. But when you tell me I'm interfering, I feel beastly.
CAROL. You are, you know.
EVELYN. There! You've done it again.
CAROL. People like Edward and me should be left to manage our own troubles.
EVELYN. All right. From now on I won't say a word.
CAROL. Cheer up.
EVELYN. I'm a blundering fool, anyhow.
CAROL. *(laughing)* Yes.
EVELYN. And instead of making you like me, I've made you laugh at me.
CAROL. That's not quite true.
EVELYN. I'm afraid it is.
CAROL. You don't know a bit what I'm really like.
EVELYN. No.
CAROL. Do you want to?
EVELYN. Yes.
CAROL. I'm not sure that's wise.
EVELYN. Why not?
CAROL. You might be shocked.
EVELYN. As bad as that?
CAROL. Yes – as bad as that.
EVELYN. I don't believe it.
CAROL. Good.
EVELYN. You're too sensitive to behave really badly.
CAROL. That's nonsense.
EVELYN. No, it isn't.

CAROL. Sensitiveness hasn't anything to do with it.
EVELYN. Yes, it has.
CAROL. Don't contradict me.
EVELYN. *(with truculence)* Why shouldn't I?
CAROL. Because it infuriates me.
EVELYN. *(slowly)* We're almost quarrelling.
CAROL. Yes.
EVELYN. I'm sorry.
CAROL. Antagonism is a bad sign.
EVELYN. What do you mean?
CAROL. *(suddenly burying her face in her hands)* Oh, Evie!
EVELYN. *(alarmed)* What on earth's the matter?
CAROL. *(muffled)* Nothing.
EVELYN. Carol, don't – please – *(He gets up and comes to her)*
CAROL. No, no. Sit down. Your man will be in in a moment,
EVELYN. Do tell me what's wrong.
CAROL. Sit down, please.
EVELYN. All right. *(He sits down)*
CAROL. Give me my bag, will you? It's over there. I want to powder my nose.

> **EVELYN** *rises. When his back is toward her, an expression of extreme satisfaction flits across* **CAROL***'s face. By the time he has turned she is once again bravely melancholy.*

EVELYN. Here. *(He gives her her bag)*
CAROL. Thank you.

> *She looks up at him with a weary smile.* **BLACKWELL** *enters and takes away the remains of the sweet.*

EVELYN. Serve the coffee at once, Blackwell; then I shan't want you any more.
BLACKWELL. Very good, sir. *(He goes out)*
CAROL. I feel better now.
EVELYN. I don't suppose you'll ever want to dine with me again.

CAROL. Don't be silly. Of course I shall.
EVELYN. I seem to have depressed you terribly.
CAROL. No – it's not your fault, really.
EVELYN. I wish I understood you a bit better.
CAROL. I'm glad you don't.

BLACKWELL *enters with coffee and liqueurs, which he places beside* EVELYN.

EVELYN. Thank you, Blackwell. Good-night.
BLACKWELL. Good-night, sir. *(He goes out.)*
EVELYN. Coffee?
CAROL. Yes, please.
EVELYN. *(pouring it out)* Sugar?
CAROL. One.
EVELYN. *(handing it to her)* There. Cointreau or brandy?
CAROL. Cointreau just a little.
EVELYN. The brandy's very good.
CAROL. All right. Brandy, then – you're so dominant.
EVELYN. Don't laugh at me any more.
CAROL. I must a little.
EVELYN. Here you are. *(He gives her some brandy and takes some himself.)*
CAROL. Next time I come I'll try to be more amusing.
EVELYN. I don't want you to be amusing if you don't feel like it.
CAROL. You're awfully kind and gentle.
EVELYN. I want you to relax completely.
CAROL. I am relaxing completely.
EVELYN. I feel you need it.
CAROL. No one else has ever taken the trouble to feel that.
EVELYN. They're all too occupied in enjoying themselves.
CAROL. But I don't think they do, really.
EVELYN. That's true, but they wouldn't dare admit it.
CAROL. Put the gramophone on.

EVELYN. Now?
CAROL. Yes, please, or I shall cry again.
EVELYN. *(rising)* What shall we have?
CAROL. Something blaring and noisy.
EVELYN. What a baby you are!
CAROL. Am I? *(He puts on a foxtrot and stands by the machine looking at her. After a pause she speaks.)* I love this tune.
EVELYN. It's not very new, I'm afraid. I must get some more of the latest ones.
CAROL. Are you ready for your lesson?
EVELYN. Lesson?
CAROL. Yes, your dancing lesson.
EVELYN. If you are.
CAROL. Of course I am! Come on. *(She rises.)*
EVELYN. I'll push the table back. *(He does so.)* There.
CAROL. Now then. *(They begin to dance.)*
EVELYN. Is the time all right?
CAROL. A scrap too fast.
EVELYN. Wait a minute. *(He stops for a second and regulates the time.)*
CAROL. That's better. *(They dance again.)*
EVELYN. I'm so sorry. Did I kick you?
CAROL. No.
EVELYN. I warned you, didn't I?
CAROL. Hold me a little tighter.
EVELYN. All right. *(They dance in silence for a moment.)*
CAROL. This is divine.
EVELYN. You're not teaching me a thing.
CAROL. You don't need it.
EVELYN. You're just being polite. I dance like an elephant.
CAROL. Don't be ridiculous. It would be terribly funny if anyone suddenly came in and found us.
EVELYN. There's not the least chance of it. *(They dance in silence for a little.)*

CAROL. Oh!
EVELYN. What is it?
CAROL. We nearly crashed into that chair.
EVELYN. I'm afraid I wasn't concentrating.
CAROL. That's very naughty of you. You must.
EVELYN. All right. *(The record comes to an end.)*
CAROL. Put on another.
EVELYN. Very well.

> *While he does so,* CAROL *looks at herself carefully in the glass over the mantelpiece.*

CAROL. I'm enjoying myself frightfully.
EVELYN. Are you, really?
CAROL. Aren't you?
EVELYN. You know I am. *(He takes her in his arms again.)*
CAROL. You really must hold me a little tighter – it's so much easier to follow.
EVELYN. Like that?
CAROL. Yes – like that.

> *They stand still, she surrendering herself to him, and holds up her face deliberately to be kissed.*

EVELYN. *(softly)* Carol!

> *He kisses her. They stand tightly clasped for a moment; then he firmly disentangles himself and turns off the gramophone.*

CAROL. *(sinking on to the sofa and passing her hand across her eyes.)* Oh, Evie!
EVELYN. *(in a different tone)* I thought so.
CAROL. *(looking up quickly)* What do you mean?
EVELYN. It's unbelievable. *(He strides about a little.)*
CAROL. *(alarmed)* What on earth are you talking about?
EVELYN. I was right. I knew it.
CAROL. *(becoming exasperated)* Knew what?
EVELYN. I'm not quite such easy game as all that.

CAROL. *(rising)* Evie!
EVELYN. What a little rotter you are.
CAROL. *(outraged)* What!!
EVELYN. Yes, you may well look surprised. I, unfortunately, am *not* surprised.
CAROL. *(after a pause)* I'm beginning to understand.
EVELYN. I'm glad.
CAROL. Very clever. I must congratulate Edward.
EVELYN. It's nothing to do with Edward.
CAROL. Liar! *(She goes and takes up her cloak.)*
EVELYN. You're not going yet.
CAROL. On the contrary, I'm going immediately.
EVELYN. Not until I choose.
CAROL. Don't speak to me like that.
EVELYN. I'm going to speak to you as you've never been spoken to before.
CAROL. Pompous ass!

She flings her cloak over her arm and goes towards the door. EVELYN *stands between her and the door.*

EVELYN. You're going to stay here.
CAROL. *(contemptuously)* Don't be so ridiculous.
EVELYN. I mean it.
CAROL. Are you quite mad?
EVELYN. No, not at all; I'm unflatteringly sane.
CAROL. Do you intend to use force to keep me here?
EVELYN. Yes, if necessary.
CAROL. Evie – what have you been reading? *(She flings down her cloak and returns to the sofa.)*
EVELYN. That's right.
CAROL. *(helping herself to a cigarette)* I always thought you were a fool.
EVELYN. Thank you. I'm sorry I was less of a fool than you hoped.
CAROL. I didn't hope for much, whatever happened.

EVELYN. You'd forgotten I was Edward's best friend.
CAROL. You're very, very sure of yourself.
EVELYN. I can afford to be. I live decently.
CAROL. Rubbish!
EVELYN. And I've got a little honour left.
CAROL. Even after living decently.
EVELYN. You would say a thing like that.
CAROL. I did.
EVELYN. I should like to say one thing –
CAROL. Please do.
EVELYN. If you and I were alone on a desert island I wouldn't touch you.
CAROL. That would be very silly of you.
EVELYN. *(rapidly losing his temper)* Haven't you any modesty or shame anywhere?
CAROL. *(smiling)* Oh dear!
EVELYN. Stop being flippant; it's only a mask to cover your humiliation.
CAROL. How discerning you are!
EVELYN. I know you much better than you think I do.
CAROL. Idiot!
EVELYN. Flinging epithets at me won't help.
CAROL. Fatuous prig.
EVELYN. Shut up.
CAROL. *(rising)* May I go now please?
EVELYN. *(almost shouting)* No.
CAROL. *(sitting down)* Very well.
EVELYN. I'm Edward's best friend.
CAROL. You've said that before.
EVELYN. And I'm damned if I'm going to stand by and see him cheapened and humiliated by you.
CAROL. You're insufferable.
EVELYN. That's beside the point.

CAROL. *(suddenly furious)* It is *not* beside the point! How dare you behave like this! If you were Edward's Siamese twin you've got no right to ask me here and insult me. You surely don't imagine that by talking until you're blue in the face you could ever alter my life one way or another. You've played a filthy second-rate trick on me and you think you did it for Edward's sake, but all the time it was only to prove to yourself how clever you are. You've got to let me go now – at once. Do you hear? If not I'll scream the place down. *(She rises and makes a dash for the door. He intercepts her. She struggles. He grasps her wrist.)* Let me go. Help! Help!

EVELYN. Shut up you little fool! *(He puts his hand over her mouth and drags her back to the sofa, upon which she collapses, sobbing.)*

CAROL. *(almost hysterical, in muffled tones)* How dare you! Oh, how dare you! It's outrageous. It's –

EVELYN. Do you want some brandy?

CAROL. Don't speak to me.

EVELYN. *(with emphasis)* Do you want some brandy?

CAROL. No.

EVELYN. You'd better have some. Stay where you are. *(He goes over and pours out a glass of brandy and brings it to her.)* Here – sit up.

CAROL. Go away. Don't come near me.

EVELYN. You're hysterical. Drink this and pull yourself together.

He puts his arm round her to lift her up. She wriggles free of him, sits up quickly by herself, snatches the glass from his hand and flings it into the fireplace.

CAROL. I don't want your filthy brandy.

EVELYN. That was childish.

CAROL. Why are you doing this to me? Why? Why? What have I ever done to you?

EVELYN. You're on the verge of ruining the life of one of the best men that ever lived.

CAROL. *(tearfully)* How?

EVELYN. You know perfectly well how.

CAROL. It's no business of yours – what I do – ever.

EVELYN. I've made it my business. What you attempted to-night with me you've accomplished with other men – you've flirted and encouraged them to make love to you, and in many cases you've given yourself to them –

CAROL. Evie!

EVELYN. I don't want you to deny it or affirm it. I *know* it's true, but I don't think Edward does; he loves you too much to believe it possible, and my object in playing on you this second-rate trick, as you call it, is to make you realise what a hideous mess you're making both of his life and your own. *(During this speech* **CAROL** *is looking at* **EVIE** *intently. He beings to stride up and down while he talks.)* Edward's too sensitive and reserved to fight for his own rights. I've known for ages that he wasn't happy – that something was weighing on his mind. To-day I asked him plump out and he admitted – (He pauses.)*

CAROL. What did he admit?

EVELYN. That he was worried and miserable about you.

CAROL. *(calmly)* And what did you advise him to do?

EVELYN. Give you hell.

CAROL. How crude of you!

EVELYN. Women of your sort require a little crudity occasionally.

CAROL. What do you mean "women of my sort"?

EVELYN. Do you want me to tell you?

CAROL. No; I don't want you to say any more at all.

EVELYN. You have the soul of a harlot.

CAROL. *(suddenly bursting out laughing)* Oh, Evie!

EVELYN. *(losing control)* Don't laugh. Don't laugh.

CAROL. *(continuing to laugh)* What do you expect me to do. You're so ridiculous –

EVELYN. I suppose you consider anyone with decent ideals ridiculous?

CAROL. *(laughing helplessly)* Oh dear! Oh dear!

EVELYN. *(working himself up more and more)* You think it funny that I should make an attempt to defend the honour of my best friend, who is too shamed by your utter wantonness to defend himself –

CAROL. *(growing hysterical)* You're mad – quite, quite mad –

EVELYN. You're deliberately ruining his reputation and wrecking his happiness because you never make the slightest effort to control your rotten passions –

CAROL. *(rising, trying to control her hysteria)* How dare you say that – how dare you –

EVELYN. Dare! I'll say it again and again. Rotten passions! All you live for, all you think of – women of your type can't exist without men – men – nothing but men all the time –

CAROL. *(frantically)* Stop! Stop! You shan't say any more. *(She gives him a ringing slap on the face. He stands quite still.)* Cad! Cad! Unutterable cad! *(She gives him another slap between each word. He remains motionless. They stand facing each other.* **CAROL** *puts her hand to her head.)* I think – I think I'm going to be ill.

She falls in a heap at his feet. He carries her back to the sofa. He deposits her there and rushes to get some more brandy. When his back is turned she lifts her head sharply and looks at him, then lets it drop attractively against the side of the sofa. He returns and ministers the brandy. After a slight pause she opens her eyes and sits up and finishes the brandy.

EVELYN. Be careful. Don't spill it on your dress.

CAROL. I'm awfully sorry to be so stupid.

EVELYN. I didn't mean to make you ill.

CAROL. *(meekly)* Please may I go home now?

EVELYN. You'd better wait a moment until you feel stronger. I won't say any more – I promise.

CAROL. My head aches.
EVELYN. Would you like some aspirin? I think I've got some somewhere.
CAROL. No, thanks.
EVELYN. It wasn't out of any personal spite, you know –
CAROL. It doesn't matter – it – *(She bursts into tears.)*
EVELYN. I say, don't cry – please.
CAROL. I can't help it. *(She cries a little more.)*
EVELYN. Please! Please!
CAROL. Leave me alone. I'll be all right in a minute.
EVELYN. I had no intention of losing my temper. I apologise.
CAROL. *(with a fresh burst of tears)* It's all so – so horrible.
EVELYN. Carol – please, please don't!
CAROL. *(sobbing bitterly)* I'd no idea – anyone could think of me like that.
EVELYN. I was only trying to show you, for Edward's sake –
CAROL. Don't – don't say any more. You promised.
EVELYN. All right, but you see I –
CAROL. I understand why you did it. It's not that I'm crying for. It's – it's – Oh God!
EVELYN. *(appealingly)* Carol –
CAROL. I'm crying because I'm so bitterly ashamed –
EVELYN. *(gently)* Carol –
CAROL. I don't want you to despise me utterly –
EVELYN. It's all right. Don't think any more about it.
CAROL. The things you've said to me are right – I have been shallow and cheap; but there's a reason that you don't know.
EVELYN. Reason?
CAROL. You've heard Edward's side of the story and you've mixed yourself up in our lives – more than ever now. It's only fair for you to hear my side, too —

EVELYN. Now look here, Carol. Don't let's say any more about it all.

CAROL. Do you mean that?

EVELYN. Yes.

CAROL. *(rising)* Very well – I suppose I deserve it. Good-night. *(She walks sadly towards the door.)*

EVELYN. Carol –

CAROL. *(turning)* Yes?

EVELYN. I'll hear your side if you want me to, but what's the use of going on any further?

CAROL. Only that unless I explain now I can never look you in the face again.

EVELYN. Carol, don't be so absurd.

CAROL. There are circumstances that justify me more than you realise.

EVELYN. Come back, then, and sit down.

CAROL. *(wearily returning)* I feel so horribly tired.

She comes back to the sofa and leans against it, looking at him. Her face is pale and she looks extremely sad and quite lovely.

EVELYN. Do sit down.

CAROL. No, but I want you to. Sit here where you needn't look at me.

EVELYN. Very well.

He sits down on the sofa and stares into the fire. CAROL *stands just behind him with her hands resting on his shoulders. Both their faces are half turned to the audience. She speaks very slowly.*

CAROL. You've been pretty brutal to me to-night and some of the hard things you said I deserve, but not all of them. I'm selfish and occasionally cheap and rather vain – and I have been unfaithful to my husband, but not before he had been unfaithful to me –

EVELYN. *(starting)* What!

CAROL. *(pressing him down)* Keep still, please. I'm telling you the truth –

EVELYN. You mean that Edward –

CAROL. I mean exactly what I say. I was completely faithful to Edward until eighteen months ago, when I discovered that he was having an affair with Zoe St. Merryn –

EVELYN. Good God! *(He moves again, but she holds him firmly.)*

CAROL. That broke me up, rather.

EVELYN. I don't believe it.

CAROL. I can't help that; it's true, all the same.

EVELYN. How did you discover it? What proof have you?

CAROL. I suspected for a little while and said nothing until I could bear it no longer; then I asked Edward and he admitted it –

EVELYN. *(twisting round)* I *must* look at you.

CAROL. *(firmly, looking into his eyes)* He admitted it.

EVELYN. It's incredible.

CAROL. Why? Edward's awfully weak and Zoe – *(she laughs sadly.)* Will you turn around again now, please. *(*EVELYN *does so and buries his face in his hands.)* Don't be upset about it, Evie – it's between Edward and me, really, and nobody knew – until now. I made him swear never to tell a soul, otherwise he'd have told you ages ago – he always tells you everything. I've behaved rather badly since then, I know, but something went dead, inside me and – well, it doesn't seem to matter much, does it?

EVELYN. *(after a pause)* May I get up now and get a drink?

CAROL. There's nothing more to say, anyhow.

    EVELYN *goes over and pours himself out a drink. He turns suddenly.*

EVELYN. You wouldn't lie to me, would you?

CAROL. *(with dignity)* Even I have a little decency left. *(She turns to go again.)*

EVELYN. Carol!

CAROL. *(turning)* Yes.
EVELYN. What can I say to you?
CAROL. Nothing.
EVELYN. I'm desperately sorry.
CAROL. All right.
EVELYN. I've been an abject, blundering fool. It wasn't my business, anyhow.
CAROL. *(with a wan smile)* Your motives were sound.
EVELYN. Can you forgive me?
CAROL. Yes, of course.
EVELYN. I mean really forgive me?
CAROL. *(holding out her hand)* Completely.
EVELYN. You're very generous. *(He takes it.)*
CAROL. There's one more thing I want to clear up.
EVELYN. What?
CAROL. I came here to-night for one reason only.
EVELYN. Yes?
CAROL. I love you!
EVELYN. *(dropping her hand)* Carol!
CAROL. It's all right – don't be afraid. I'm going now – but I didn't want you to think me too cheap – that's all.
EVELYN. I'm utterly bewildered.
CAROL. It hasn't been very easy for either of us, has it?
EVELYN. You can't mean what you say.
CAROL. You know I do – you've known it all along, subconsciously.
EVELYN. Carol – I'm dreadfully – horribly embarrassed.
CAROL. Poor old Evie.
EVELYN. I don't know what to do.
CAROL. We'll both laugh over to-night one day, won't we?
EVELYN. Will we?
CAROL. *(with beautifully forced gaiety)* Yes – you see.
EVELYN. You are an extraordinary woman.
CAROL. Just rather silly, I'm afraid. Good-night.

EVELYN. I'm going to see you home.
CAROL. No, please. I'd rather go alone. Please, I mean it, honestly.
EVELYN. But –
CAROL. It's only just round the corner.
EVELYN. I can't let you go alone.
CAROL. *(with gentle firmness)* You must – please.
EVELYN. *(looking down)* All right.
CAROL. We're friends, aren't we?
EVELYN. *(still looking down)* Yes.
CAROL. In spite of everything?
EVELYN. Yes.
CAROL. Because of everything?
EVELYN. Oh, Carol!
CAROL. Good-night, my dear. *(She comes to him and kisses him gently on the mouth. After a moment she disentangles herself.)* No, no! I didn't mean it, really. I'm not going to be cheap any more. Stand quite still where you are, not looking. I don't want you to move until I've gone.

She goes out quietly, leaving him standing stock-still. After a moment the front door slams. EVELYN *turns in the direction of the sound.*

EVELYN. *(emotionally)* Carol – Oh God!

He goes over to the sofa and flings himself down on it, with his face buried in his hands. CAROL *comes softly in again. Her cloak is over her arm. She gives one look in his direction and then goes noiselessly into his bedroom, closing the door after her.*

CURTAIN

ACT III

The scene is the same as Act I. It is about twelve o'clock in the morning. One night has elapsed since Act II.)

When the curtain rises the studio is empty. There is the sound of the front door bell ringing with some violence. **BERRY** *enters, R., and crosses over L. He exits and reappears in a moment, ushering in* **EVELYN**. **EVELYN** *is looking extremely white and strained.*

BERRY. Can I offer you anything to drink, sir?
EVELYN. No, thanks.
BERRY. The master's sure to be in soon, sir.
EVELYN. All right, thanks.
BERRY. He's only taking a walk in the Park.
EVELYN. I think I will have a drink, after all.
BERRY. Very good, sir. Whisky and soda?
EVELYN. Yes, please.

BERRY goes out. EVELYN proceeds to pace up and down the room a little. BERRY returns with a whisky and soda.

Oh, thanks. *(He takes it.)*

BERRY. Would you like the papers, sir, or have you seen them already?
EVELYN. I've seen them, thanks.
BERRY. Shall I tell Mrs Churt that you are here, sir?
EVELYN. No – no. Please don't disturb her.
BERRY. Very good, sir.

He goes out again. **EVELYN** *once more proceeds to pace up and down with the whisky and soda in his hand. He is obviously extremely agitated. After a moment* **CAROL** *enters from R. She looks fresh and charming. She gives a slight start on seeing* **EVELYN**.

CAROL. Evie!

EVELYN. *(jumping – he turns)* I've come to see Edward.

CAROL. What's the matter?

EVELYN. I've come to see Edward.

CAROL. *(with faint apprehension)* I know – you just said so. Aren't you going to say good morning?

EVELYN. Good morning.

CAROL. *(going over to him)* No more than that?

EVELYN. No – no more. *(He turns away.)*

CAROL. *(biting her lip)* I see.

EVELYN. I want to see him alone.

CAROL. *(putting her hand on his arm)* Evie, what's wrong?

EVELYN. You can seriously ask me that?

CAROL. Why are you behaving like this?

EVELYN. *(turning away)* You're hopeless.

CAROL. You're not going to do anything foolish, are you?

EVELYN. I'm going to do the only thing possible.

CAROL. *(swinging him round)* Evie!

EVELYN. Leave me alone.

CAROL. But listen –

EVELYN. *(wrenching himself free from her)* Don't touch me, please.

CAROL. *(pleading)* Evie – please – why are you being so horrid?

EVELYN. I don't want to look at you – or see you again ever!

CAROL. Why – why – what have I done?

EVELYN. *(sinking into a chair with his face in his hands)* Leave me alone. Leave me alone.

CAROL. You don't love me at all, then?

EVELYN. For God's sake stop!

CAROL. You don't – you don't –

EVELYN. Shut up! Shut up!

CAROL. You coward! *(She goes over to the window.)*
EVELYN. Please go away. You'll only make everything much worse.
CAROL. Why have you come here this morning?
EVELYN. To tell Edward about last night.
CAROL. What will you tell him?
EVELYN. The truth.
CAROL. You're insane.
EVELYN. I was – but I'm not any more.
CAROL. *(coming quickly back to him)* You can't mean this.
EVELYN. I do mean it.
CAROL. But why! Why!! Why!!!
EVELYN. I don't expect you to understand.
CAROL. Evie, listen. Be sensible for a moment.
EVELYN. It's no use going on like that. I've made up my mind.
CAROL. Evie –
EVELYN. *(rising)* Go away! Go away!
CAROL. *(following him)* I love you.
EVELYN. Be quiet.
CAROL. I love you – I love you. Tell what you like – shout it from the housetops. I love you!
EVELYN. *(catching hold of her)* Shut up – you must. Someone will hear.
CAROL. I don't care.
EVELYN. You don't love me – you never did for a moment – it was all a trick.
CAROL. *(outraged)* Evie!
EVELYN. I can see it all now – I can see it all.
CAROL. You're talking nonsense.
EVELYN. For God's sake go away from me.
CAROL. *(helplessly)* I don't know what to do.
EVELYN. Leave me alone. I've got to tell Edward the truth.
CAROL. In heaven's name, why?

EVELYN. Can't you see why?
CAROL. No. What good will it do?
EVELYN. I've betrayed him.
CAROL. That's no reason for you to betray me as well.
EVELYN. He trusted me – completely.
CAROL. Well, why not let him go on trusting you?
EVELYN. Because I'm unworthy of it for ever.
CAROL. And what about me?
EVELYN. It was your fault.
CAROL. How chivalrous.
EVELYN. You lied to me.
CAROL. *(firmly)* I did *not* lie to you.
EVELYN. You said you came last night because you loved me.
CAROL. So I did!
EVELYN. You came out of curiosity and stayed out of revenge.
CAROL. What a fool you are!
EVELYN. You determined to get even with me.
CAROL. Evie!
EVELYN. It's true – it's true – you know it is.
CAROL. Why have you built up this ridiculous story in your mind?
EVELYN. It's true.
CAROL. *(with great firmness)* It's nothing of the sort, and if you calm yourself and think seriously for a moment, you'll realise the complete absurdity of it. You must be sensible. Do you hear – you *must* be sensible. You're on the verge of wrecking everything out of sheer hysteria.
EVELYN. Everything is wrecked already. I've got nothing left – no honour, no decency –
CAROL. *(quietly)* I gave myself to you last night, Evie –
EVELYN. Don't – don't –

CAROL. I gave myself to you completely and for one reason only – I loved you. I love you now.

EVELYN. Carol, please –

CAROL. If you tell Edward – I shall go away and never see either of you again.

EVELYN. I can't help it. I –

CAROL. You *can* help it. What you're contemplating is utterly without reason. If you're trying to vindicate your honour, you can't seriously achieve it by betraying mine. We've both behaved abominably, I admit. We've both been weak and uncontrolled and given way completely and we shall suffer for it accordingly, you needn't doubt that for a minute. We're in a terrible mess, but we're in it together and together we must remain –

EVELYN. I shall never be able to look Edward in the face again.

CAROL. Will you be able to face him any better after you've told him?

EVELYN. Yes.

CAROL. Why?

EVELYN. Because I shall have done the only decent thing left to me.

CAROL. You'll only succeed in making him suffer as well as yourself and me. Can't you see the uselessness of it?

EVELYN. I can't see him and talk to him with this shame between us.

CAROL. You must – so must I. It's the just penalty for what we've done. You said just now you never wanted to see me again. Well, I promise you you never shall – alone. You at least can go away. I can't – I've got to stay and get through the next few months as best I can –

There comes a ring at the front door bell.

EVELYN. *(pacing the room)* O God! What am I to do?

CAROL. *(quickly)* Nothing – nothing yet, anyhow. Think sensibly and quietly – everything depends on you keeping calm –

   BERRY *enters and crosses over L. and exits.*

EVELYN. Is that Edward?

CAROL. Yes, I expect so. He's always forgetting his key.

EVELYN. *(terribly undecided)* Carol, I –

CAROL. Promise you'll do nothing yet.

EVELYN. I can't – I –

CAROL. *(whispering violently)* Promise me – wait a little – promise me. Will you promise me?

EVELYN. *(helplessly)* Yes.

   BERRY *re-enters.*

BERRY. *(announcing)* Mrs St. Merryn.

   ZOE *enters briskly.*

ZOE. Good morning, Carol. I haven't seen you for months. How are you?

CAROL. *(as they kiss)* Splendid. I heard you were back.

ZOE. Hallo, Evie!

EVELYN. *(coldly)* Good morning.

ZOE. I gather that Edward is expected?

CAROL. Yes, he'll be back any minute.

EVELYN. Good-bye.

   He goes out abruptly.

ZOE. *(surprised)* That was one of the most sudden exits I've ever seen.

CAROL. *(carelessly)* I think Evie's upset about something.

ZOE. I didn't think he was capable of it.

CAROL. *(conventionally)* Are you glad to be back?

ZOE. Delighted. London's looking so pretty with all the roads up.

CAROL. *(absently)* Are they? I hadn't noticed.

ZOE. I don't see how you could fail to unless you travel exclusively in the underground.
CAROL. Where are you staying?
ZOE. Claridge's.
CAROL. Oh!
ZOE. It's so beautifully austere.
CAROL. What?
ZOE. *(patiently)* I said it was so beautifully austere.
CAROL. Oh yes, it is.
ZOE. You're looking awfully well.
CAROL. I am, frightfully well.
ZOE. Don't you think I'm looking frightfully well?
CAROL. Yes, you certainly are. Travelling obviously agrees with you.
ZOE. It's so comforting to know that we both look so awfully well. Can I have a cigarette?
CAROL. Yes, of course. I'm so sorry. Here – *(She hands her a box open)*
ZOE. Thank you, dear. There aren't any in this box, but it doesn't matter.
CAROL. How annoying! Wait a minute. *(She takes another box off a table, L.)* Here –
ZOE. *(taking one)* You seem a little distrait this morning, if I may say so.
CAROL. I've got rather a headache.
ZOE. I'm so sorry. You don't look very well.
CAROL. I think, if you'll forgive me, I'll go and take some aspirin.
ZOE. Of course. I should lie down until lunch if I were you.
CAROL. Perhaps I will. Edward's certain to be in soon.
ZOE. I'll be perfectly happy waiting.
CAROL. You must come and dine one night.
ZOE. I'd adore to.
CAROL. Good-bye for the present, dear. *(She kisses her.)*

ZOE. Good-bye. I'm sorry you're so seedy. I'm afraid you've been overdoing it lately.

CAROL. *(irritatedly)* Overdoing what?

ZOE. *(vaguely)* Oh, everything.

CAROL. No, I haven't.

ZOE. I'm so glad.

> CAROL *goes out.* ZOE *wanders round the room, smiling to herself, examining various portraits, etc.*
>
> *After a moment* EDWARD *enters.*

EDWARD. Zoe! How long have you been here?

ZOE. Only a few minutes.

EDWARD. I've been out in the Park.

ZOE. I didn't know it was still there.

EDWARD. I'm afraid you're finding the old town sadly changed.

ZOE. I'm sure it's much more hygienic now.

EDWARD. Have you seen Carol?

ZOE. Yes. She's just gone to bed.

EDWARD. Gone to bed?

ZOE. She said she had a headache.

EDWARD. How do you think she's looking?

ZOE. *(laughing)* Awfully well.

EDWARD. What are you laughing at?

ZOE. Carol always makes me laugh.

EDWARD. Why?

ZOE. She's so consistent.

EDWARD. Are you lunching with me?

ZOE. If you like. I've got to go to Sloane Street first and look at Mary Phillip's house. She wants to let it to me.

EDWARD. Pick me up here on the way back.

ZOE. I really came to ask you to dine to-night and go to a play.

EDWARD. I'd love to. What do you want to see?

ZOE. A nice clean play, please, Edward.
EDWARD. Splendid. We shan't have any trouble getting seats.
ZOE. I'm so old-fashioned – I like love stories without the slightest suggestion of sex.
EDWARD. You ought to be a critic.
ZOE. You're an awfully nice person to come back to!
EDWARD. *(smiling)* Am I?
ZOE. Yes. One picks up the threads exactly where they were dropped.
EDWARD. They were never dropped.
ZOE. Carol's an awful fool.
EDWARD. Why?
ZOE. She could hold you if she wanted to.
EDWARD. Don't be tiresome, Zoe.
ZOE. What are you going to do about it?
EDWARD. About what?
ZOE. Do you really want me to be explicit?
EDWARD. No. I know perfectly well what you mean.
ZOE. You're wasting time.
EDWARD. Not at all. I'm working hard.
ZOE. You said that yesterday and it was no more convincing then than it is now.
EDWARD. It's true.
ZOE. Perhaps, but rather beside the point.
EDWARD. What is the point?
ZOE. Your happiness.
EDWARD. What beautiful thoughts you have, Zoe.
ZOE. Don't be flippant.
EDWARD. Flippancy alleviates my boredom with the whole subject.
ZOE. Are you sure you're not confusing boredom with lack of moral courage?
EDWARD. Possibly.

ZOE. Well, don't.
EDWARD. I refuse to be dominated, Zoe – even by you!
ZOE. *(smiling)* That's right, dear.
EDWARD. And don't laugh at me.
ZOE. I always have. I fail to see why I should stop now.
EDWARD. I resent it bitterly.
ZOE. Dear Edward.
EDWARD. What do you expect me to do?
ZOE. Deliver an ultimatum.
EDWARD. That would be stepping out of my character.
ZOE. Nonsense!
EDWARD. I am essentially a weak-minded man.
ZOE. Nothing of the sort – you're a lazy idealist.
EDWARD. That sounds delightful.
ZOE. So it is in theory; in practice it's sterility personified.
EDWARD. You're terribly didactic.
ZOE. I'm trying to rouse you.
EDWARD. Why?
ZOE. Because you're discontented and unhappy.
EDWARD. I never said so.
ZOE. You don't need to – it's written all over you.
EDWARD. You think I'd be happier if I bashed about making scenes and delivering ultimatums?
ZOE. Certainly – you at least might achieve something.
EDWARD. What, for instance?
ZOE. Freedom!
EDWARD. That's a myth.
ZOE. Oh no, it isn't.
EDWARD. In this case it's impossible.
ZOE. Why?
EDWARD. *(turning away)* Oh, don't let's discuss it any more.
ZOE. You *are* annoying, Edward.
EDWARD. Evie went on like that for hours yesterday.

ZOE. Evie?
EDWARD. Yes. He seemed to advocate violence as being the best method.
ZOE. He would.
EDWARD. He even offered to teach Carol a lesson.
ZOE. What sort of lesson?
EDWARD. He didn't explain.
ZOE. Poor Evie.
EDWARD. You needn't despise him so utterly. He's a good sort.
ZOE. He's the quintessence of masculine complacency.
EDWARD. I'm sure it's a great comfort to him. I wish I was.
ZOE. Evie will get into trouble one of these days. He's too worldly.
EDWARD. If I were free, Zoe, would you marry me?
ZOE. Edward!
EDWARD. I suddenly thought of it.
ZOE. *(laughing)* This is terribly sudden.
EDWARD. Don't be silly.
ZOE. You must give me time to think.
EDWARD. Do shut up and be serious.
ZOE. I have a vague feeling that your proposal is a little previous.
EDWARD. It wasn't a proposal – just an idea.
ZOE. Not exactly an original one. We discussed it all ages ago.
EDWARD. And whose fault was it that it never came off?
ZOE. *(promptly)* Yours.
EDWARD. Zoe, how can you? It was entirely yours.
ZOE. Nonsense! I was dead set on it.
EDWARD. You refused me and rushed off to Africa.
ZOE. You can't call Algiers Africa.
EDWARD. It is, all the same.
ZOE. If you'd loved me enough, you'd have followed me.

EDWARD. I was waiting for you to come back.
ZOE. Let's stop talking about it – it's rather painful.
EDWARD. We weren't in love, really, anyhow.
ZOE. Weren't we?
EDWARD. I don't know.
ZOE. It's all very difficult.
EDWARD. Yes.
ZOE. I think I shall go away again soon.
EDWARD. Oh, Zoe, please don't.
ZOE. It's going to be awkward if I stay.
EDWARD. No, it isn't.
ZOE. We're both on rather dangerous ground.
EDWARD. I don't see why.
ZOE. Yes, you do, perfectly.
EDWARD. I do not.
ZOE. If I stay, we shall probably fall in love properly – we're both at a perilous age.
EDWARD. What if we do?
ZOE. It would be too horrible, with all this Carol business going on and everything.
EDWARD. You're crossing your bridges before you come to them.
ZOE. I shall go, all the same.
EDWARD. That is rank cowardice.
ZOE. No, it isn't; it's sound sense.
EDWARD. It will be beastly for you.
ZOE. Not so beastly as if I stayed, really – in the long run.
EDWARD. What could happen?
ZOE. Oh, the usual thing, I suppose – we should have an affair and spoil everything.
EDWARD. I don't see why.
ZOE. You're being very obstinate this morning.
EDWARD. If I were in love with you at all, it would be in a very nice, restrained way.

ZOE. We should both tire of that very quickly.
EDWARD. Zoe, how can you be so unpleasant?
ZOE. I'm only facing facts.
EDWARD. We've been together a good deal in the past.
ZOE. I know.
EDWARD. And everything was above reproach.
ZOE. Entirely.
EDWARD. Well, why can't we go on like that?
ZOE. Because even if we do, people will say we don't.
EDWARD. What does that matter?
ZOE. It matters a lot. I've had enough squalor in the past few years to last me for life.
EDWARD. Yes, but I don't see –
ZOE. Also I have a strange aversion to coming between man and wife.
EDWARD. Oh, shut up, Zoe.
ZOE. It's true. I suffer from a pre-war conscience.
EDWARD. There's no question of that, really.
ZOE. Don't be silly. Of course there is.
EDWARD. Carol wouldn't care.
ZOE. What difference does that make? Really, Edward, you're being horribly flaccid over the whole thing!
EDWARD. Don't lets argue about it.
ZOE. All right.
EDWARD. But please don't go away again – just yet.
ZOE. I'll think it over, Edward.
EDWARD. You've depressed me terribly.
ZOE. I'm sorry.
EDWARD. It's all such a hopeless muddle.
ZOE. It needn't be.
EDWARD. I'd no idea you were so designing.
ZOE. What a horrid thing to say!
EDWARD. It's true though, isn't it?
ZOE. Absolutely.

EDWARD. Oh, Zoe –
ZOE. I must go.
EDWARD. Remember lunch.
ZOE. I'll pick you up here.
EDWARD. No, don't – I'll meet you.
ZOE. Where?
EDWARD. Berkeley – one o'clock.
ZOE. I'm sure to be late.
EDWARD. So am I.
ZOE. Good-bye, dear. *(She goes up to him and kisses him lightly.)*
EDWARD. Zoe!
ZOE. That was part of the design!

> *She goes out.* EDWARD *walks up and down irritably for a moment, then lights a cigarette and flings himself into an arm-chair. The telephone rings. He gives an exclamation of annoyance and rises to answer it.*

EDWARD. *(at telephone)* Hallo!… Yes – yes… Who is it speaking?… No, I'm afraid you can't. She isn't very well –

> CAROL *enters in time to catch the last sentence.*

CAROL. Who is it?
EDWARD. Oh… hold on, please… Harry Challoner *(He hands her the telephone curtly and goes over to the window.)*
CAROL. *(at telephone)* Hallo!… Yes, it's me… No – no, I can't. I'm sorry… All right, if you like… I'll be in between six and seven… Yes… Good-bye.

> *She hangs up the receiver and looks toward* EDWARD *who has his back turned. She is about to go out again, when he turns.*

EDWARD. Carol.
CAROL. Yes?
EDWARD. I want to talk to you.
CAROL. Is anything the matter?
EDWARD. Yes. Sit down, will you?

CAROL. *(sitting)* If you like.
EDWARD. I want to get things settled.
CAROL. Get things settled?
EDWARD. Yes.
CAROL. What sort of things?
EDWARD. Our exact relationship.
CAROL. What *do* you mean?
EDWARD. Just that.
CAROL. I don't understand.
EDWARD. I think you do.
CAROL. *(by now extremely apprehensive)* I don't Edward, honestly.
EDWARD. Do you intend to pursue your present course indefinitely?
CAROL. What are you talking about?
EDWARD. Infidelity.
CAROL. Are you insinuating that I –
EDWARD. I'm insinuating nothing. I'm stating that you have been unfaithful to me.
CAROL. *(rising)* Edward!
EDWARD. *(firmly)* Sit down. This is not a scene – it's a process of readjustment. Please let us keep it as brief as possible.
CAROL. *(sinking down)* How can you be so horrible?
EDWARD. Do you deny it?
CAROL. Of course I do.
EDWARD. Carol, let me disillusion you. I'm not bluffing. I *know*. I've known for ages. It's no use wasting time denying and arguing. We must decide what's to be done about it.
CAROL. How can you be so foul!
EDWARD. *(wearily)* Oh, Carol, do stop acting.
CAROL. You're insufferable.
EDWARD. Once and for all will you be sensible?

CAROL. I hate you.

EDWARD. That would be beautifully definite if you weren't so unreliable.

CAROL. Do you want me to hate you?

EDWARD. To be honest with you, I really don't mind.

CAROL. *(outraged)* Edward!

EDWARD. Don't be a fool, Carol.

CAROL. How dare you! How dare you!

EDWARD. We will face facts, please.

CAROL. *(rising)* I'm not going to stay here and be insulted.

EDWARD. You're not being insulted – it's I who have been insulted. You've been publicly underrating my intelligence for months.

CAROL. That's what's upsetting you, is it?

EDWARD. Certainly it is. I wish you'd sit down.

CAROL. I'm going to my room.

EDWARD. You're only temporarily evading the issues by doing that.

CAROL. What's the object of all this?

EDWARD. The object, as I said before, is to get our relationship satisfactorily defined.

CAROL. *(with grandeur)* It's satisfactorily defined now as far as I am concerned.

EDWARD. I would prefer the satisfaction to be mutual.

CAROL. You think you're very clever, don't you?

EDWARD. What a common remark! You'll be sticking your tongue out at me in a minute.

CAROL. I suppose Zoe has been putting you up to this.

EDWARD. Meaning that I have no initiative of my own anyhow?

CAROL. Exactly.

EDWARD. That's charming of you – and fits in beautifully with your behaviour during the last year.

CAROL. Are you in love with me still?

EDWARD. Do you expect me to be?
CAROL. Are you?
EDWARD. No, Carol.
CAROL. I see.
EDWARD. All of which is beside the point.
CAROL. No, it isn't. If you loved me you'd never say such things to me.
EDWARD. I admit that it would be more comfortable for you if I just suffered and suffered in silence.
CAROL. You're too unemotional to be capable of any suffering.
EDWARD. Do you imagine you're putting up a good defence for yourself?
CAROL. I'm not attempting to.
EDWARD. That brings us to my ultimatum.
CAROL. *(with a forced laugh)* Ultimatum! Really Edward!
EDWARD. You've been unfaithful to me three times during the past year – Maurice Verney, Geoffrey Poole, and now Harry Challoner!
CAROL. *(blanching slightly)* Edward!
EDWARD. All three married men, which adds considerably to the general sordidness of the whole business.
CAROL. *(losing control)* I will *not* be spoken to like this!
EDWARD. *(with sudden force)* Be quiet! Do you still deny it?
CAROL. *(more dimly)* No.
EDWARD. That's better.
CAROL. *(sullenly)* I'm sorry.
EDWARD. That's too sudden to be convincing.
CAROL. *(breaking up slightly; after a long pause)* What are you going to do?
EDWARD. Wait until next time.
CAROL. Next time?
EDWARD. Yes.
CAROL. And what then?

EDWARD. I shall divorce you.

CAROL. Edward!

EDWARD. I mean it. Whether the man happens to be married or single will not make the slightest difference.

CAROL. *(looking down)* I see.

EDWARD. Is that quite clear?

CAROL. Quite.

EDWARD. Incidentally, I wish you to give up Harry Challoner entirely. I object to you even being seen with such a second-rate bounder.

CAROL. *(looking at him)* Very well.

EDWARD. We'll both do our best to forget the whole thing. We can get along perfectly well together with a little effort.

CAROL. There's no more, is there?

EDWARD. No, that's all.

CAROL goes slowly towards the door in silence. Her expression is very thoughtful. When she reaches the door she turns.

CAROL. *(in a different voice)* Edward.

EDWARD. Yes?

CAROL. Please forgive me.

EDWARD. Forgiveness in this case is surely rather unimportant.

CAROL. Oh, please, please – *(She bursts into tears and goes towards him.)*

EDWARD. Now then, Carol –

CAROL. *(standing in front of him weeping)* You must forgive me – you must!

EDWARD. All right.

CAROL. I didn't love any of them – I swear I didn't.

EDWARD. *(turning away irritably)* Oh, Carol –

CAROL. You've been utterly indifferent to me for ages.

EDWARD. Naturally.

CAROL. No, but before – I mean before – last year you stopped loving me.
EDWARD. Please don't go on like this.
CAROL. It's true – it's true. I was lonely.
EDWARD. Don't talk such utter nonsense.
CAROL. *(working herself up)* It isn't nonsense – it's you I love really all the time. I hate Harry Challoner, really. I've been trying to break with him for ages. I made a vow weeks ago that I'd never be unfaithful to you again – honestly I did, I swear it. I'm sick of everybody. I wanted to ask you to take me away abroad somewhere, but I didn't dare – you had so much work to do – and you were so cold and horrid. Edward – Edward – you've got to love me again – you must. I shall go mad if you don't. Please – Edward darling. *(She flings herself into his arms.)*
EDWARD. *(gently disentangling himself)* There now – it's all right. Do stop. *(He kisses her dutifully)*
CAROL. I feel so bitterly ashamed.
EDWARD. Stop crying.
CAROL. I swear I'll be good. I swear I will.
EDWARD. That's right. Now control yourself.
CAROL. I'll never see Harry again.
EDWARD. Very well. For heaven's sake stop crying.
CAROL. I do love you really, you know. That's what makes it so awful.
EDWARD. Pull yourself together.
CAROL. *(dabbing her eyes)* I'll try.
EDWARD. Go and lie down and take something.
CAROL. What shall I take?
EDWARD. Aspirin, I should think.
CAROL. I had some just now.
EDWARD. Have some more.
CAROL. All right. Oh, God!

She goes out slowly, still half sobbing. **EDWARD** *heaves a sigh of mingled relief and irritation, he again flings himself into an arm-chair. Then comes the sound of the front door bell. He groans.* **BERRY** *enters from R.*

EDWARD. Whoever it is, Berry, I'm out.

BERRY. Very good, sir. *(He goes out L. After a moment he re-enters.)* I'm very sorry, sir; it's Major Bathurst. The porter downstairs told him you'd just come in; he's called already this morning.

EDWARD. Nobody told me. You'd better show him in.

BERRY. Yes, sir. *(He goes out and returns, announcing)* Major Bathurst.

EVELYN *comes in. He looks more harassed than ever.* **BERRY** *goes out.*

EDWARD. Hallo, Evie!

EVELYN. *(haltingly)* Edward – I – I've come to say good-bye.

EDWARD. *(surprised)* Good-bye?

EVELYN. Yes. I came earlier this morning, but you were out.

EDWARD. But where on earth are you going?

EVELYN. Australia.

EDWARD. Why Australia?

EVELYN. *(weakly)* I've always wanted to go to Australia.

EDWARD. What *do* you mean?

EVELYN. I mean I've got to go there on business.

EDWARD. It's very sudden, isn't it?

EVELYN. Yes. I had a wire from my brother.

EDWARD. I didn't know he was in Australia.

EVELYN. He isn't. He's in Cheltenham, but he sent me a wire saying I ought to go out there at once.

EDWARD. What's the matter with you, Evie?

EVELYN. Nothing.

EDWARD. You're not only telling me extremely fatuous lies, but you look like death.

EVELYN. They're not lies. I –

EDWARD. Don't be an ass. Have a drink.
EVELYN. No – I don't want a drink.
EDWARD. What's wrong?
EVELYN. There's nothing wrong.
EDWARD. You'd better tell me, you know.
EVELYN. I want to tell you.
EDWARD. Come on, then.
EVELYN. I've got to tell you.
EDWARD. Out with it.
EVELYN. But I can't.
EDWARD. Surely that's rather silly.
EVELYN. I tried to shoot myself this morning.
EDWARD. You what!!!
EVELYN. Tried to shoot myself.
EDWARD. *(alarmed)* In God's name, why?
EVELYN. *(brokenly)* Oh, Edward.
EDWARD. Evie, what *has* happened?
EVELYN. I'm the filthiest cad in the world.
EDWARD. Don't be ridiculous.
EVELYN. Our friendship is over for ever.
EDWARD. *(with irritation)* Do stop all this melodrama, Evie, and tell me what's the matter.
EVELYN. I've betrayed you, utterly.
EDWARD. *(in great astonishment)* Betrayed *me*?
EVELYN. *(looking down)* Yes.
EDWARD. How?
EVELYN. *(brokenly)* Carol!
EDWARD. Carol! Well, what about her?
EVELYN. Carol dined with me last night.
EDWARD. Oh, did she?
EVELYN. And – and – O my God! *(He sinks into a chair by the table and leans his head on his arms.)*
EDWARD. *(in amazement)* You don't seriously mean to tell me –

EVELYN. *(in muffled tones)* Yes.
EDWARD. You and Carol!
EVELYN. Yes.
EDWARD. This is too much! *(He bursts out laughing.)*
EVELYN. *(looking up astounded)* Edward!
EDWARD. I can't bear it. *(He laughs louder.)*
EVELYN. *(rising)* Edward – old man – please –
EDWARD. *(helplessly)* It's unbelievable – incredible. Oh dear! *(He collapses on the window seat.)*
EVELYN. *(approaching him)* Edward – for God's sake –
EDWARD. *(weakly)* Don't come near me, I shall be all right in a minute.
EVELYN. *(with growing anger)* You must be mad.
EDWARD. I certainly feel very strange. *(He goes into fits of laughter again.)*
EVELYN. *(outraged)* Edward – do you realise what I've just told you?
EDWARD. *(trying to control himself)* Yes – perfectly.
EVELYN. And you can laugh!
EDWARD. Will you hand me a cigarette, please?
EVELYN. *(irately)* Look here, Edward –
EDWARD. *(with sudden firmness)* Will you hand me a cigarette, please.
EVELYN. Here. *(He offers him his case.)*
EDWARD. Thanks *(He takes one.)* Light.
EVELYN. Here. *(He strikes a match.)*
EDWARD. Thanks. I feel better now.
EVELYN. Well! What are you going to do about it?
EDWARD. Ring that bell, will you? By the door.
EVELYN. I can find my own way out.
EDWARD. *(firmly)* You're not going yet. Ring the bell, please.

    EVELYN *looks at him and then goes and rings the bell.*

EVELYN. Look here, Edward, I came here this morning because I felt I owed it to our friendship to confess the truth to you –

EDWARD. You're out of your depth, Evie – far, far out of your depth.

EVELYN. I don't know what you mean.

EDWARD. This is reality, not fiction.

BERRY *enters.*

BERRY. You rang, sir?

EDWARD. Will you ask your mistress to come down immediately, please, Berry? It's very important.

BERRY. Yes, sir. *(He goes out.)*

EVELYN. *(panic-stricken)* Edward, this is not fair of you.

EDWARD. *(unceremoniously)* Shut up.

EVELYN. This is between us.

EDWARD. The three of us, Evie – what's known, I believe, as the eternal triangle.

EVELYN. Let me tell you one thing – what happened was not deliberate.

EDWARD. You prefer to be thought a fool rather than a cad!

EVELYN. Yes, if you like to put it that way,

EDWARD. How typical!

EVELYN. I only asked Carol to dine, in the first place, for your sake.

EDWARD. For my sake?

EVELYN. Yes, I intended to teach her a lesson.

EDWARD. And she ended up by teaching you one.

EVELYN. *(utterly shocked)* Edward!

EDWARD. Men of your sort should stick to athletics and not attempt physiology.

EVELYN. I deserve that.

EDWARD. *(agreeably)* Fully.

CAROL *enters from R. She starts visibly on seeing* EVELYN.

CAROL. What's the matter?

EDWARD. Don't look so surprised, Carol. It's terribly irritating.

CAROL. I don't understand.

EDWARD. I gather that you and Evie –

EVELYN. *(wounded by such frankness)* Edward!

CAROL. *(looking at* EVELYN*)* You cad!

EDWARD. It was very unpleasant of you, Carol –

CAROL. *(appealingly)* Edward, please –

EDWARD. I should like to know how it all happened.

EVELYN. I told you – I –

EDWARD. Carol, will you explain, please?

CAROL. Certainly not.

EDWARD. Very well. You must allow me to reconstruct it for myself.

EVELYN. Surely this is unnecessary.

EDWARD. That is entirely for me to decide.

CAROL. You're being unbelievably cheap.

EDWARD. *(mildly)* Really, Carol – keep a slight grip on your values.

EVELYN. Say what you like. I don't care.

EDWARD. It wouldn't make the slightest difference if you did.

EVELYN. Damned ungenerous.

EDWARD. Shut up and don't be an ass. You and Carol have brought about this abominable situation. It's up to you to keep quiet and let me straighten it out in my own way.

EVELYN. *(turning away)* Very well.

EDWARD. Thank you. Now then – Evie, you asked Carol to dine with you alone at your flat?

EVELYN. Yes.

EDWARD. Why?

EVELYN. I told you.

EDWARD. In order to teach her a lesson.
CAROL. Oh, this is insufferable.
EDWARD. You're perfectly right, it is. I gather that the first part of the lesson, Evie, necessitated you making love to her. Am I right?
EVELYN. *(impatiently)* Oh yes –
EDWARD. And then what? *(Turning.)*
EVELYN. Look here, Edward, I'm damned if I'm going to listen to this any longer –
CAROL. Neither am I!
EDWARD. Tell me the truth, then, Carol. It will simplify matters considerably. Do you love Evie?
CAROL. No.
EDWARD. Then why, if it's not an indelicate question, did you –
CAROL. *(violently)* Because he insulted me and tried to humiliate me and I determined to show him that he wasn't as clever as he thought he was.
EDWARD. Admirable. You, Evie, had the ineffable conceit to pit your meagre experience of the world against an extremely attractive and obviously unscrupulous woman. You then give in to her completely despite the fact that she is the wife of your friend; and not content with that, you turn on her afterward, work yourself up into a frenzy of false melodramatic values, rush round here and blurt it out to me doubtless under the delusion that by uncovering the whole shameful business you are vindicating your own honour! Oh, Evie, what a pitiful fool you are!
EVELYN. It's no use blackguarding me any more, is it? What are you going to do about it?
EDWARD. I don't quite know yet.
CAROL. There's nothing to be done.
EDWARD. You're too sure of yourself, Carol – you always have been.
EVELYN. I wish to God I had shot myself.

EDWARD. It's a little late to think of that now.

EVELYN. You're being unnecessarily cruel, Edward.

EDWARD. I'm afraid I'm a bitter disappointment to you both. You see emotionally I'm unmoved. The capacity for feeling very deeply over Carol died a long while ago.

EVELYN. I should have thought that for the sake of our friendship –

EDWARD. That's sheer cant. You've considerably over-estimated our friendship for years. If you care to analyse it honestly you'll discover that we both bore one another stiff and always have. We were at school together – in different forms – since when we've dined together on an average of once a month. We've confided our troubles superficially for the want of something to talk about. We're poles apart mentally and physically; we've built up this so-called great friendship on a basis of false tradition, and the only reason I realised it first is because my brain functions quicker than yours –

EVELYN. *(shattered)* Edward!

EDWARD. And I should like to add – having naturally a more acute sense of sex psychology than you – that the reason you took such a fatal interest in Carol's morals was not on my account at all, but because she's snubbed you severely several times and you were probably very much attracted to her.

EVELYN. It's not true. You're disgusting.

EDWARD. Be that as it may, the solution to the whole thing is obvious.

EVELYN. What do you mean?

EDWARD. I'll tell you. Carol you must go away immediately.

CAROL. *(horrified)* Edward –

EVELYN. *(stricken)* But – I – I –

EDWARD. Wait a moment. Let me explain. Carol, you and I have no longer the slightest justification for living together. If you go away abroad somewhere I will make it perfectly easy for you to divorce me. If you don't agree to this, I shall file a petition against you at once, naming Evie as co-respondent. That's the second ultimatum I've delivered this morning and I'm feeling extremely tired. *(He sits down.)*

CAROL. Edward, you can't mean this – you can't.

EDWARD. I do. I mean it more than I've ever meant anything in my life.

CAROL. *(bursting into tears of rage)* I won't stand it. I won't!

EDWARD. You're not being very polite to Evie.

EVELYN. You think you're being damned clever.

EDWARD. That's been hurled at me so often just lately that I'm honestly beginning to believe I am.

CAROL. You utter beast.

EDWARD. Well – what's the decision?

CAROL. *(wailing)* I'll never speak to you again – never – never – never.

EDWARD. *(rising)* Evie?

EVELYN. *(gruffly)* You'd better give us time to think.

EDWARD. What is the time now, anyhow?

EVELYN. *(looking at his watch)* Twenty-past one.

EDWARD. My God! I knew I should be late. I'll be at the Berkeley if you want me.

> EDWARD *goes out.* EVELYN *and* CAROL *look after him and then at each other.* CAROL *after a pause walks over and sits next to* EVIE.

CAROL. Evie.

EVIE. What?

CAROL. *(sweetly)* There's still time for you to shoot yourself!

CURTAIN

www.ingramcontent.com/pod-product-compliance
Ingram Content Group UK Ltd.
Pitfield, Milton Keynes, MK11 3LW, UK
UKHW021844210426
5322IPUK00022B/456